THERAPY WITH INFANTS

THERAPY WITH INFANTS
Treating a Traumatised Child

Inger Thormann and
Inger Poulsen

Translated by Dorte H. Silver

R Routledge
Taylor & Francis Group

LONDON AND NEW YORK

First published 2016 by Karnac Books Ltd.

Published 2018 by Routledge
2 Park Square, Milton Park, Abingdon, Oxon OX14 4RN
711 Third Avenue, New York, NY 10017, USA

Routledge is an imprint of the Taylor & Francis Group, an informa business

British Library Cataloguing in Publication Data

A C.I.P. for this book is available from the British Library

ISBN-13: 9781782203094 (pbk)

Typeset by V Publishing Solutions Pvt Ltd., Chennai, India

CONTENTS

ABOUT THE AUTHORS

Inger Thormann, MA, qualified from the Danish Supervisory Board of Psychological Practice in 1997 and has worked since 1973 as a psychologist in residential facilities for children who have suffered neglect and abuse, at the Skodsborg Treatment Centre for Infants. She is the author of six books for professionals and six children's books, and is active as a film consultant, lecturer and teacher. She is also a sychologist in private practice.

Inger Poulsen is trained in body/gestalt therapy, Sandplay therapy, and psychotherapy. She has worked with child, adolescent and adult psychology and psychiatry in Denmark, Sweden and Greenland. Since 1997 she has been head of The Family House, a psychotherapy clinic for pregnant women and families with young children. She is a psychologist in private practice offering infant therapy, early trauma therapy for older children, as well as therapy for adults who have experienced early (pre-language) trauma. She is also active as a speaker, teacher and supervisor for professionals in Denmark and Greenland.

FOREWORD

Our current time calls for evidence-based knowledge, meaning that everything we do should be validated by research findings. We want evidence to ensure that what we are doing actually works. The efficacy of therapy, however, is difficult to verify scientifically, because therapy is never the sole factor determining the outcome. There are always other concomitant factors affecting a person. That is also the case for therapy with infants. When a young child receives therapy, the child often also receives more attention—or more focused attention—from his or her caregivers. The therapy may lead to greater awareness in the caregiver, which in turn leads to improved care or added attention. This makes it difficult to verify scientific evidence for the efficacy of therapy. However, individual examples make a strong case, and an analysis of case stories may serve as a convincing illustration of the efficacy of the method that characterises infant therapy. The child is in crisis; the child undergoes infant therapy; the child improves.

We have worked with infant therapy since 1998 in residential/ hospital settings, with day patients and in private practice. We have worked with children from birth to three years, and we have used the method with older children, adolescents, and adults. We think it is time to share our experiences.

Our work began with a specific case concerning a six-month-old girl who was referred to The Family House. The little girl was traumatised after physical abuse from her father, and when she was referred she had six bone fractures. She was a very serious and withdrawn little girl, and it was obvious that both she and her mother needed help. Child Protective Services (CPS) referred the girl for therapy. At the time, the method applied in infant therapy was not integrated into the work at The Family House, and CPS therefore made a referral to the observation and treatment centre Skodsborg Treatment Centre for Infants (in short: Skodsborg).

At Skodsborg, "putting emotions into words" with the children we worked with was a practice we had applied for years, and we were familiar with Françoise Dolto's theories about the importance of verbal communication with children of all ages. However, it was the invitation to review a recently published book by Dolto's student Caroline Eliacheff that produced the spark which eventually made infant therapy an integrated part of the treatment approach at Skodsborg. Since 1998, all children referred to Skodsborg have received infant therapy as a natural part of their treatment.

A productive collaboration developed between our two treatment centres and ourselves, the authors of this book, and we saw the benefits of our respective approaches to therapy with infants and toddlers. Skodsborg offers residential treatment to children in crisis. The child's primary caregiver here is a trained educator who always works as part of an interdisciplinary team. The child's parents play a key role in the treatment, although, for a variety of reasons, the referring authorities have deemed them incapable of caring for their child.

The Family House offers individual and group-based family therapy on an out-patient basis, provided by trained psychotherapists. The interventions take place both at The Family House and in the family's own home, typically when there is a risk that a child may have to be removed from the home. After the specific case with the six-month-old girl, we and our respective facilities continued our cooperation, and together we have developed the method that characterises infant therapy as it is practised in Denmark today.

Infant therapy is aimed at traumatised children from birth to three years. Dolto suggests that a trauma occurring before a child has fully developed language requires special attention, and that the child is able to benefit from a therapy process where the traumatic situation is put into words. Dolto also found that the method is helpful for older children, adolescents, and adults who have experienced trauma during the pre-verbal phase of their lives. In our practice, we have countless examples that the method can be successful in helping people of all ages achieve a new understanding of the factors that have acted as barriers to certain aspects of their development.

When we speak of and practise therapy with infants our main sources of inspiration are Françoise Dolto's and Caroline Eliacheff's work. However, other theorists have provided additional inspiration and even become our "mentors", and it would be unthinkable to discuss our work with traumatised children without mentioning them. The attachment between child and caregiver is crucial, so of course we must mention John Bowlby, the founder of attachment theory. Similarly, it is impossible to work with infants and young children in crisis without drawing on Donald Winnicott and his theories of transitional objects and phenomena. Development psychology as described by Daniel Stern is also a constant companion in our work, just as several Danish psychologists have made important contributions to our current professional framework, including Susan Hart's work on neuropsychology and Per Schultz Jørgensen's understanding of the interaction between protective and stress factors, vulnerability and risk. Chapter Five was inspired in part by the work of psychotherapist Susanne Bundgaard.

We have divided the book into two parts. Part I deals with infants and toddlers, and Part II discusses the application of the method with older children, adolescents, and adults and how other professions can use the method in day-to-day situations.

We have given case stories a prominent role in the book, in part to make the theories easier to relate to the reader's everyday practice. The examples come from our own work experience and have been anonymised to protect the identity of the individual clients.

We have both found our work with children and families profoundly inspiring, and with this book we hope to share this inspiration with the readers.

Last but by no means least, we wish to thank our close colleagues at Skodsborg and The Family House in Horsens. A special thanks goes to Julie Eldrup and Elsebeth Willemann for their support in the process of writing this book. We thank the children, young people, and adults who have contributed to the book with their life stories. And we thank Per Schultz Jørgensen for collegial inspiration, Ole Gammeltoft for untiring support and Susan Hart for productive discussions about the young child's ability to understand communication. Finally, we thank the foundation Aase og Ejnar Danielsens Fond whose kind support enabled us to take a working residence at the retreat Refugiet Klitgården.

Inger Thormann and Inger Poulsen

PART I

CHAPTER ONE

Presentation of Françoise Dolto and Caroline Eliacheff

Françoise Dolto

Françoise Dolto (1908–1988) was a paediatrician and psychoanalyst who worked for forty years at Trousseau Hospital in Paris. In addition to her work at the hospital, once a week she saw children in her private clinic in Rue Cujas. In several regards, this work put Dolto in a unique position. In her own perception, her clinical work was not based primarily on conceptual knowledge but on the individual children that she worked with. To her, the main source of knowledge was first-hand experience. The children provided her insight and her knowledge, and that has lent her words particular gravity.

In her work with the children, she relied on words as well as things like crayons and modelling clay. No case was without hope, no situation was impervious to improvement. Her open-mindedness was unique. She once said, "There is no fixed limit for what can be cured nor any norm for the depth of our understanding" (Dolto, 1988, p. 12) [translated for this edition].

At her clinic, Dolto saw children had who given up any hope that they might be seen by others, met with their pain and receive vital care. She saw children with arrested development, emotionally frustrated children, children without language, psychotic, and mentally ill children. She saw these children's pain and their symptoms as the results of adults' failure to understand the children as independent individuals with their own needs and longings. At a very early stage, she decided to be the children's advocate, both in her therapeutic work and in society.

Dolto was above all a practitioner; she carried out clinical work with children and youths, and this practical clinical work was always her first priority. In her work she made numerous observations, and over her many years of practice these observations came to serve as the basis for research studies, which in turn led to the development of theories. Dolto wanted to share her experiences with the public, with French families and expectant parents. She wanted to help parents understand their children better and teach them to see life through the eyes of their child. To this end, for example, she did weekly radio broadcasts where parents could send in questions which she would reply to on the air. She wrote articles for newspapers and popular magazines, and she was recognised and loved. At one point she was deemed to be among the four most popular women in France, ahead of women like Brigitte Bardot and Catherine Deneuve. This illustrates her success in making the general population take an interest in the child as an independent individual, a member of a family. Her insights and knowledge were respected by "the people".

Dolto not only took an interest in children's lives but also in the lives of the mothers. In the 1960s and 1970s, more and more women entered the job market, and the children were placed in various forms of day care. This new situation required adjustment from both the mother and the child. Dolto had the idea for "The Green Houses", which offered a setting for "separation and reunion" but also for "the child in a learning and socialisation process". The Green Houses gave both children and parents an opportunity to prepare for the new conditions with support from professionals. To this day, there are Green Houses all over France (see below).

The core of Dolto's work was that one should *never allow the child's pain to be forgotten*. Well ahead of her time, Dolto made this point as early as 1948. She was a contemporary of John Bowlby's, Réne Spitz's and other key figures focusing on attachment and separation issues between child and caregiver. In a groundbreaking shift in perspective, they saw the young child as an independent individual, a person separate from the mother. Dolto treated the child as a responsible and independent person, who was born into this world with his or her own subjectivity and desires. She considered and accommodated the needs of the child's family. Dolto saw it as her most pressing task to find means and words to soothe the traumatised child's pain and bring the child back on a dynamic development path.

Dolto worked with the parents to understand the events what had occurred in the child's life. The parents might be plagued by painful, repressed experiences that affected the communication in the family and were in turn expressed, in an altered form, in the child's symptoms. This finding might lead to questions about the parents' responsibility for the child's wellbeing, health, and development and about the guilt that parents feel when their child is not thriving. About this, Dolto says, "To blame the parents, who are already suffering by seeing their child's suffering, would be completely misguided" (1998, p. 14) [translated for this edition].

Relationships can generate healthy or pathological states. The therapist needs to understand the relationships within the family in order to promote healing. To help the parents, the therapist needs to tell them how the issues are interconnected, which is not the same as telling them that they have done something wrong. When dealing with unconscious acts, it makes no sense to speak about guilt; rather, it is a matter of misunderstandings with adverse consequences. It is important to say things as they are, also in cases where the parents have done everything they could, with the best intentions, and where the truth may be perceived as both hurtful and painful.

"The truth has a structuring and healing impact on the mind, and the truth has the capacity to dissolve the symptom" (Dolto, 1998, p. 15) [translated for this edition]. Dolto was convinced that a child's neurotic or psychotic disorder is related to untruths and things that have been left unsaid, even when this cover-up was thought to be in the best interest of the child. Dolto saw no difference between children and adults in therapy and psychoanalysis, despite the different settings. To Dolto, the child's own desire to undergo therapy was important, so she introduced a symbolic fee, where children above a certain age have to bring along a token payment, for example a postage stamp or a pebble, to signify that the child is here for his or her own sake.

Dolto's clinical work with children and adults was based on the key notion that inside the body of every human being is a desiring subject, however hidden and unheard—even in newborn infants who have chosen to survive despite difficult odds. Consistent with this belief, she also worked with infants in her clinic, which was unheard of at the time. Many analysts observed her consultations and received their training as psychoanalysts from her; one of them was Caroline Eliacheff.

The Green Houses

With the Green Houses, which were founded in the 1970s, Dolto wanted to create a setting where children and parents could learn to adjust to the new situation where they were separated for several hours every day, as more and more mothers worked away from home. The Green Houses were not about childcare or observation but a venue where children and parents could experience what Dolto felt ought to take place before the child was placed in day care, nursery, or preschool: a place for play and for a "meeting", where the child was treated as an independent individual.

Dolto was especially interested in children from birth until one and half years of age. She saw how receptive and open to communication children are, and she saw and understood the mother's feelings of guilt for having to leave her children in someone else's care. Dolto helped the mother by addressing the child in the mother's presence:

> When your mummy drops you off in the morning she does it because she has to go to work, just as she did while you were in her womb. Back then, you were with mummy when she went to work. Now that you have been born, you can't go with mummy to work, because you have to be with children your own age. Other adults will be here to look after you, just as we look after all the children, and you are going to be away from your mummy most of the day, because she is going to be at work. (Dolto, 1993, p. 378) [translated for this edition]

Dolto was convinced that children hear and understand everything we tell them, and that newborn infants understand all languages. Only after a few months does the child's understanding narrow to the mother tongue.

> He understands that we speak to him as a person about the crisis that awaits him. He feels safe when he hears us tell him that the crisis is a sign that he loves his mother, and that he is loved by her, just

as he loves his father and is loved by him. (ibid, p. 379) [translated for this edition]

The parents have brought the child into the world, and they go to work to provide for them. At the Green Houses, the parents learn how they should greet the child when they return after six to eight hours.

> When you pick him up from the nursery, don't smother him with hugs and kisses. Instead, talk to him, and talk to the person who has been looking after him while you were away. Get him dressed, with love and tenderness, remain calm, and don't give in to the urge to hug and kiss him. To an infant, six to eight hours is like a week to an adult, so in a sense, he has "forgotten" you. He doesn't understand what is going on, because he is in a different mood. (ibid, p. 379) [translated for this edition]
>
> When he feels the urge, he will grasp at his bottle. If you smother him, he seems like something you eat, like the baby's bottle. He feels that you are swallowing him. Instead, you should gently guide him into the mood that characterises your relationship with him. Speak to him, dress him, and take him home. Then you can shower him with kisses. (ibid, p. 379) [translated for this edition]

The mothers who have been to the Green Houses say that it is amazing to see the difference between the children in nursery school who have been to one of the Green Houses and the ones who have not. The unprepared children cry when their mother leaves, and they cry when she returns. That is their only way to release the tension, whether it stems from joy or from pain. In any case, they feel insecure.

When children attend nursery school, they encounter other children's aggressions. These aggressions are less of a challenge for the child, however, if the child is secure in the knowledge that his or her mother is always there, introjected into the child, providing a sense of security. However, for the child to feel this sense of security—the sense of security that the mother represents to the child—the mother must be a compassionate witness to the child's struggles and experiences, and she has to comfort the child. She has to observe, as the child repeatedly encounters dangerous challenges while she is present, free of anxiety, and she has to speak with the child about the dangers that the child is going to encounter. The mother also has to support the child by using the right words to talk about real dangers. The dangers that the child encounters are often insignificant, but they may have far-reaching consequences for a child who has not received this kind of support.

After a few days at the Green House, the parents begin to see significant changes in their child and in the child's relationship with his mother, indeed, both parents; at this point they are convinced that the infant actually understands language. They discover that they can speak to the child about what the child has experienced during the day and about what is happening in the child's life in general.

Dolto said,

> Man is, from birth, a linguistic being. The child is born with a linguistic joy potential that we can either support or deny. If this joy is not nurtured through language, the symbolic function, which is always active when we are awake, will be idling. It lacks code and fails to organise a language for communication. (1998, p. 17) [translated for this edition]

It may seem hard to believe that an infant is able to understand language, even before he or she is able to produce sounds that we perceive as words, but anyone who engages with an infant and is able to interpret the child's mimicry will see that the child responds to everything. At the Green Houses, not only the child's own mother but the other mothers too become aware of the child's expressive mimicry.

Case: Julian

Dolto relates how a woman came in with a three-month-old child. The mother said, "I'm going to leave him here. I'm just going across the street to do some shopping". This was the woman's first visit to the Green House, and Dolto said to her, "You can't leave your child here. No one leaves their child here." "But I'm just going across the street." "Well, then you have to dress him and take him with you. Then you can both come back." "If that's how it's going to be, I'm not going to come back at all." "You do what you want to, but you're not leaving Julian".

Dolto describes that when the mother said that she was going to leave him behind, the child's face clearly showed that he was scared that his mother would abandon him. She was the only familiar person to him in the world, and she was going to leave him in an unfamiliar place only minutes after they had arrived. Dolto said to her, "Look at his reaction". "It's probably just a coincidence", the mother replied. But both she and the other mothers saw the child's reaction. Regardless, the mother insisted that it was a coincidence. Dolto said to the child, "Please understand that your mother is going to leave with you. She may come back here, but she's taking you with her. No one leaves their child here". The boy calmed down and looked at his mother with a pleased look.

The mother stayed at the Green House. As the evening drew near, she said to the other mothers, "I get it now; it's amazing. At first I wasn't even considering coming back. I felt that Dolto was attacking me, but now I see that she said what she said for the sake of my child. It's amazing that such a young child can understand language".

At the Green Houses, the children not only learn about "separation and reunion"; they also undergo a "learning and socialisation process". Dolto wanted to prepare the child to enter society, which has rules and norms for acceptable behaviour, and she pointed out that the parents need to help their child accept these rules.

In Dolto's time, the Green Houses only had two rules: When you play with water, you have to wear an apron; when you ride your bicycle indoors, you are not allowed to cross the red line on the floor. Both rules were sensible, as the apron kept the children's clothes from getting soaked, and the red line marked the border to the baby area. When a child encountered these restrictions in spontaneous play, many reacted by throwing a temper tantrum, and the parents, mostly the mothers, had to help their child understand that this was the way it was. This was clearly a preparation for life outside the home. Dolto felt that the Green Houses were needed not only to help mothers and children find appropriate rituals for saying hello and goodbye but also to keep hold of themselves in relation to the demands that they would inevitably face when the child had to go into day care, and the mother had to go to work.

Françoise Dolto's theoretical contribution

Françoise Dolto's theories mainly concern infants aged nought to one and a half years and the child's parents and are based on the work of

Sigmund Freud, Jacques Lacan, and Melanie Klein. While Melanie Klein focused on the clinical work with children with psychoses and severe disorders, Dolto focused on everyday psychopathology and thus the problems she encountered in her daily work as a paediatrician. That is the area that is reflected in her concepts and theories. However, her clinical experience with children with psychoses and autism and with infants with any conceivable difficulty or impairment also informed her theoretical contributions.

> It's all about communication ... Even in the womb, human beings strive to communicate. It is this interpersonal relationship that makes the child human. The newborn child recognises the mother on her voice and scent. The mother addresses her baby with words that translate the child's emotions, suffering and history and give the child access to the human code of language (ibid, p. 17) [translated for this edition].

Dolto emphasises the importance of continuity in interpersonal relationships. Only in the relationship with another person can the child find a reason for existing. From day one, the child is symbolically embedded in a new relationship, a triangle, through the mother's conscious or unconscious communication with the father. The father's role in the triangle differs radically from the mother's. It is "separating" and liberates the child from a regressive relationship with the mother or her substitute.

The need for both sexes in creating new life should be verbally explained to the child, Dolto argued. A woman can only become a mother with a man's involvement. Thus, the infant exists in a triangular relationship from birth, indeed, in a sense, even from conception. Even if the mother's relationship with the child appears to dominate the child's world at first, it would be harmful for the child to remain in this position as the object of the mother's most profound desire. It is therefore important for the mother to gradually direct her erotic desires elsewhere. "Any situation where the child serves as a prosthesis for one of the parents is perverting" (ibid, p. 18) [translated for this edition].

Dolto's most important theoretical contributions address the "meeting" between child and caregiver, communication and symbolic castration, that is, boundaries in relation to "the other".

Françoise Dolto's early inspiration

A brief look at Dolto's own childhood reveals certain groundbreaking experiences for Françoise as a child and young girl; experiences that appear to be at the root of her later life choices, in both her personal and professional life. Already as a child, Françoise declared that she wanted to be a paediatrician. In her own words, she wanted to be a "parenting doctor". She wanted to educate parents and families because she saw the need for advice in her own family.

Françoise was born in 1908. She grew up in a bourgeois Parisian family. The woman's place was in the home, and women were discouraged from seeking an education. Outwardly, the family—mother, father and three children—was the image of love and tenderness, but behind the facade, the family environment was steeped in anti-German feelings, racism, and anti-Semitism.

Françoise was very close to her Irish nursemaid. Later, however, the parents discovered that the nursemaid was a heroin addict, and that she had taken Françoise with her to a high-end brothel. The maid was immediately dismissed, and so Françoise experienced the devastating loss of a person she loved dearly. Another crucial experience was the loss of her big sister to cancer when Françoise was twelve years old. The mother, who was very close to her oldest daughter, gave Françoise the impression that she could have saved her sister's life, had she only prayed more fervently for her recovery. At one point, Françoise's younger brother developed stomach aches, lost his appetite and stopped eating. Françoise saw that the basis for his behaviour was tension among the servants in the household. The doctor was called to the house and prescribed a diet for the boy. He did not ask any questions about what had transpired in the family prior to the eating disorder. Françoise had observed that the nursemaid was angry with the kitchen maid, and the boy found himself in this field of tension and reacted to the conflict.

At twenty years of age, Françoise had a very negative self-image and struggled with depression and feelings of guilt. She saw her symptoms as reactions to the constant pressures she was under. She struggled to break free of the rules and norms that held her back. The main priority for her parents was to find her a husband who would provide for her, while Françoise's main priority was to have the education she so passionately wanted. During her medical studies she underwent three years of psychoanalysis. She viewed these three years as a life-changing miracle. Her early notions of becoming a "parenting doctor" took on substance. She wanted to work as a paediatrician, utilising the experiences she had earned in her own psychoanalysis. She saw how most doctors were unable to link affective events with physiological symptoms and was determined to use psychoanalysis to prevent health problems in children.

Françoise Dolto achieved the goals she had set for her professional life. She became a "parenting doctor", as she had wanted since childhood, and she conveyed her experiences to French parents. Françoise Dolto's husband, Boris Dolto, was a physician and a physiotherapist. He shared his profound knowledge of the language of the body with his wife. In relation to infants and children who have not yet acquired a language to be able to speak their mind, this insight into the language of the body is a crucial tool for the therapist.

Caroline Eliacheff

Caroline Eliacheff (b. 1947) is a student of Françoise Dolto's, and in her professional capacity she observed Dolto's clinical work every Thursday in her clinic at Rue Cujas. She is herself a trained physician, child psychiatrist, and psychoanalyst. After working in a children's hospital on the outskirts of Paris for fifteen years she came to work at the orphanage Paul-Manchon in Antony, Paris, where Françoise Dolto had been seeing children since 1973.

Like Françoise Dolto, Caroline Eliacheff points out that she is the child's therapist, not their caregiver. Her role is not to show compassion, comfort or remedy the calamities that have occurred in the child's life. Instead, as the child's therapist she has to enable her clients to represent their suffering in symbolic form and transform them into psychological experiences that they can bring with them as they move forward in life.

Also like Françoise Dolto, Caroline Eliacheff is convinced that children are born with an innate language and thus also the ability to perceive and understand words. Eliacheff (1994) describes how everything that is left unsaid disrupts the symbolisation process, or, as we have paraphrased this essential insight in our work: Everything that is left unsaid ties up energy. The emphasis is on the words that are spoken to the child. The words address the child's history, the parents, the life in the womb, the circumstances, and the child's present and future situation.

The infants that Caroline Eliacheff treats have all experienced very stressful events and situations and disrupted contact. The children's reactions to these traumas are expressed in somatic disorders, including vomiting, diarrhoea, breathing difficulties, and infections. Through these somatic disorders, the children communicate their psychological crisis, their grief, and their abandonment. The children rely on this "somatic language" because they have not yet mastered the verbal language. Caroline Eliacheff believes that the child's somatic symptoms carry symbolic meaning. The symptom points to the painful experiences and disruptions that the child has been exposed to, and which are integrated into the child's unconscious mind. Therapy/psychoanalysis makes it possible to relate the child's story to the child, to put the child's experiences of loss and disrupted contact into words and to convey the caused of these experiences. This therapeutic verbalisation lets the child relive the events and process grief, for example, over losing both birth parents. She believes that everything that is left unsaid causes a cleavage in the symbolisation process, which is initially expressed in the form of somatic symptoms. If the stressful experiences are not put into words, the symptoms become ingrained.

In her assumption about the capacity of words to unlock unconscious material, Caroline Eliacheff sympathises with the general theories about crisis resolution that are used with older children, adolescents, and adults. The new and remarkable aspect from our perspective is her experiences with and knowledge about infants' capacity for benefiting from crisis therapy, even before they have acquired the means for expressing themselves verbally. The following case excerpts illustrate how Caroline Eliacheff interprets infants' symbolic language and puts events into words.

Case: Oliver

Oliver was two and half months old when his therapy began. He had lived at the infant orphanage Paul-Manchon since he was twelve days old. Oliver was his mother's ninth child, and during the pregnancy she had decided that she would give the child up for adoption. Both the staff in the maternity ward and at the orphanage had a good impression of the mother, and everybody thought or hoped that she would change her mind, although no one talked about this openly.

As the staff realised that the mother was sticking to her decision, Oliver fell ill. He developed a serious case of dermatitis in his face and scalp, and his airways became clogged, causing laboured breathing. In his first therapy session he was crying and generally in a miserable condition. His primary caregiver summed up his brief life story so far, in his presence. After the story he stopped crying, and Caroline Eliacheff addressed him directly, saying, "You have a good and brave mother. She knows that she can't take care of you as well as she would like, and therefore she has made the decision that she thinks is best for you: that you should grow up in a family who will be your adoptive family. The people who are looking after you right now have held on to the hope, without telling you, that your mother might change her mind, and perhaps they have caused you to share this hope. Now they have realised what a good and kind person your mother is. What she is saying is true. For your own sake, she wants you to grow up in another family, who will take you in. It is her wish that this family should not have the same colour skin as you, black skin. We are not sure if that is how it's going to be. But you don't need to change the colour of your skin. You will always be the son of the man and the woman who conceived you, your birth parents, who will always remain the same". (Eliacheff, 1994, p. 23) [translated for this edition]

One week later, the therapist and Oliver met again. His skin problem was gone, but his breathing was still laboured. In this session, Caroline said him, "You are having difficulty breathing, perhaps because you wish to return to the time when you were in your mother's womb and weren't breathing—before you were separated from her. But if you have decided to live you will have to breathe. You carry your mother from that time inside you, in your heart. You were not separated from her because you began to breathe, and you will not be returned to her because you stop breathing". When Caroline Eliacheff stopped speaking to Oliver she found to her amazement that his airways were clear, and that he was breathing through his nose.

Therapeutic reflections

When Caroline Eliacheff chose these particular words, her choice was based in part on the following therapeutic considerations: In her assessment, however qualified Oliver's caregivers were, they inadvertently did him harm because of the sympathy they felt for his mother and because of their ideas about what characterises a "good mother"—which includes not abandoning one's child. When they finally did address this in words, the staff realised that they had probably regarded their wishful thinking as real. This was when Oliver developed dermatitis. The timing made the therapist wonder if Oliver might be carefully observing his mother's wish: that he would be adopted by a family with a different skin colour than his own. For Oliver to adopt the family in a healthy rather than a regressive manner, he needed to know that his birth parents lived on inside him—that they were an integrated part of his body.

Oliver's breathing difficulties too were seen as symptomatic of disruption in his life, a sudden sense of emptiness. While his caregivers still believed that his birth mother would return he must have felt very close to them, without the emptiness that a sudden separation always causes. However, the moment when the caregivers realised that the separation and the resulting emptiness would in fact occur, Oliver sought to recreate the state of complete bodily integration he had known in his mother's womb, a time when he was not alone, and when his lungs were not yet working. This illustrates how important it is to express the physical separation in words.

In all her case stories, Caroline Eliacheff emphasises the importance of close cooperation between herself and the professional staff at the orphanage. The primary caregiver takes part in all the therapy sessions with the child, and he or she is the one who relates the child's history and the child's life at the orphanage. In their everyday interactions outside the therapy sessions, the caregiver verbally repeats the therapist's interpretation of the child's symptoms to the child. The collaboration between therapist and caregiver is therefore a crucial condition for a successful outcome.

Only the most severely affected children are seen by Caroline Eliacheff. In most cases, the primary caregiver consults her and subsequently meets the child with important words about the child's history and current life. In some cases, this is sufficient; in other cases, Caroline Eliacheff sees the child at a later time. That was the case with Fleur.

Case: Fleur

On a cool day, a little girl was discovered lying in a park inside a garbage bag, wrapped in a pink blanket. She was taken to hospital where they measured her body temperature to 35.5 degrees Celsius. She weighed 2,600 grams and her left collar bone was fractured. Thirteen days after she was found, she was transferred to the infant orphanage. When she arrived there she appeared to be doing well, and she continued to do well during her first month at the orphanage. Meanwhile, police was trying to identify and locate the mother.

Suddenly, Fleur's condition changed. She developed a bad cough, and her airways were clogged; when she suddenly stopped breathing entirely she was rushed to the hospital and put into intensive care. Her primary caregiver at the orphanage, who visited daily, found her to be very weak and often with a rigidly arched back. Deeply concerned, the caregiver consulted with Caroline Eliacheff, who listened to Fleur's life story. She asked the caregiver to address the following points with Fleur:

- talk about her birth (due to her body posture and her neck, which she had arched during birth) in order to tell her that they did not know the circumstances about her birth; further, the caregiver should tell Fleur about how she was found;
- tell her that her mother had handed her over to society alive, and that Fleur had kept herself alive;
- explain to her that no one knew at this point whether she would ever see the mother who gave birth to her, but that the police were looking for her;
- tell her that the staff could not tell whether she wanted to live or die; let her know that her decision would be respected but not in the hospital, since hospital doctors are obligated to prevent children from dying;
- explain to her that she carries her mother inside her, and that the staff thought that her lung condition may be her way of making the mother live inside her, the way she had been when they were both connected through the placenta.

The caregiver later returned and said that she had spoken with Fleur while the girl was asleep. She woke up just before the caregiver left and held her in an intense gaze. To the doctors' surprise, Fleur soon improved, and two days later she was able to leave the intensive care unit. After returning to the orphanage, however, Fleur continued to express an inner disharmony through diarrhoea, breathing difficulties, and vomiting.

Every two weeks she underwent psychoanalysis with Caroline Eliacheff. In these sessions Eliacheff emphasised to Fleur that her mother had not yet been located; that she thought Fleur might be trying to hold on to her mother with her lungs while letting go of her with her diarrhoea, but that whatever she did, her mother would always be inside her. Fleur listened with rapt attention. As the therapy progressed, there continued to be many somatic symptoms, but Fleur's overall condition improved. When she came in for her final sessions at the age of five months she was accompanied by her adoptive parents. She now clearly demonstrated that she had chosen life.

In this case, Caroline Eliacheff made a point of telling Fleur that she may die if that is her personal wish, because this also implies that she may live despite having been separated from the source of her life.

Understanding the infant's competences

For centuries, adults have not attributed human emotions to children until they could speak, and assumed that they only had access to fairly rudimentary means of expressing their most basic needs. Even after children have acquired language, their capacity for understanding is not acknowledged, especially when it does not suit the adult. Most, if not all, psychologists/therapists/psychoanalysts will have encountered parents who share grim family stories in the presence of a child, perhaps even a child over six years of age, while the adults claim that the child knows nothing about this since he or she is too young to understand.

Caroline Eliacheff has followed the advances in our understanding of infants' and young children's competences, and she does not think that it is a coincidence that psychoanalysts are the ones to insist that language makes sense to human beings right from birth.

By viewing the infant as a subject who begins to exist and react as a human being rather than an immature animal, psychoanalysis questions how it has been possible, for so long, to perpetuate the notion of the infant as incapable of understanding. Understanding is a complex process, but thanks to theories and analytical practice with adults and children we have learned to form a concept of the psychological activity in very young children.

Immediately after birth, the child lets his or her voice be heard, is given a name and hears speech all around. This embeds the child in a social existence and in symbolic activity. The symbolic activity in a child who has not yet acquired speech is expressed through bodily functions that require no learning, such as breathing, digestion, immune system responses, sensory impressions, and other expressions. Because the child is exposed to language, the child's body is capable of expressing more than just biological functions. Remarkably, when we seek to attribute symbolic meaning to somatic health problems in children (which does not rule out medical treatment when necessary), we are often the first to be amazed to see how the health problem disappears. It almost seems as if language acts as an "organiser" that positions elements and alters and manipulates conditions for biological as well as psychological functioning.

Among those who acknowledge that infants and young children understand what we tell them about their origins or about the causes of a disrupted relationship, some wonder whether we should tell the child everything, or whether there are things we should "protect" the child from. Adults and adolescents who have been subjected to unexpected "disclosures" about their origins, parents or ancestors, often find that once the initial shock has settled, the fact that the truth has been *spoken* has enabled them to recall all sorts of memories, fragments of conversations, opinions that were perceived but not interpreted, somatic representations, often crucial decisions that were made in complete ignorance and incompatible pieces of a puzzle where a missing piece kept them from seeing the big picture.

Children, and not only those who are removed from the home, are exposed to varying degrees of suffering, injustice, disease, or death, and psychoanalysis does not spare them of any aspects of life. This enables them, together with the analyst/therapist, to recall the moods that accompanied the event or the words that were said, moods that the child can then accept to leave behind, such as they are, as the memories of a distant past.

Via their work, Françoise Dolto and Caroline Eliacheff, teacher and student, have inspired us both to embrace a different mindset and a different daily practice.

CHAPTER TWO

Infant therapy in practice at Skodsborg treatment centre for infants

Prior to 1998 we had no known practice for psychoanalysis and/or therapy with infants at the Skodsborg Treatment Centre for Infants (Skodsborg). We did *speak* with the infants. We told them things, we listened to them and we engaged the children in dialogue. We also saw the impact of the dialogue on the child and found that "speaking with" an infant is essential and necessary. Previously, at Skodsborg we mainly used words as an educational tool. We did not refer to our work with children under the age of two and a half years as "therapy" or "psychoanalysis". With children of this age and older, we speak of play therapy, which is provided by the psychologist. However, based on our cumulative theoretical and practical experiences we have been using the term "infant therapy" for years.

At Skodsborg, our infant therapy practice is quite similar to Caroline Eliacheff's practice. Due to practical circumstances, the children already know me (IT), and unlike Dolto and Eliacheff I have my office in the building where the children live, so when the individual child comes in for a therapy session, he or she simply goes from the residential section to my therapy room. Sometimes I choose to perform the therapy in the child's familiar surroundings. The child's primary caregiver is always present during the therapy, and conversations about the process occur both prior to and during the sessions. As the in-house psychologist, I already know the child's history and the symptoms the child displays to his or her caregivers. Therefore I begin the therapy process by telling the child what I know, and what the caregiver has told me. It is a judgment call whether the child needs actual therapy, or whether the efforts of the caregiver, with support from the psychologist, are enough. Typically, I see the child because the caregivers have a shared concern about the child's development, and the decision whether to arrange therapy for the child is then made in the larger team involved with the child.

Case: Simone

Background

Simone's mother was a thirty-year-old middle-class woman, and she was born in a hospital in Copenhagen. For a few years, the woman had had a mixed substance abuse problem, and Simone was born with withdrawal symptoms. She stayed in hospital for five and a half weeks and underwent detoxification with the aid of Phenemal and opium drops. When she was ready to be released from hospital she was referred to Skodsborg.

As we got to know mother and child, we saw a good connection between them, which they had developed during their stay in hospital. At Skodsborg, the mother initially visited her daughter every day; later, the arrangement was changed to three visits a week. We saw a very special intensity in the mother–child relationship, and Simone was radiant in the dialogues with her mother. A couple of times during the first ten months of Simone's life, the mother would fail to show up for a week or more, and then she would return. Every time, Simone reacted with sadness—a sadness that melted away when she saw her mother again.

Simone's crisis

When Simone was thirteen months old the mother failed to show up after not missing a single visit for three months. This time, Simone's reaction was very strong. She was extremely sad and distressed. She sat on the floor, staring blankly into space. She severed all contact with her caregivers. At mealtimes, she was placed in her seat at the table, but she was unable to eat or drink. Her sleep was fitful and interrupted. No one knew the mother's whereabouts.

After three days, Simone's primary caregiver, Susan, came to see me (IT). She was very concerned and asked for help. The staff in her section had done all they could to assist Simone and help her hold on to the hope that her mother would return. They had shown her extra care and had put her feelings of abandonment and concern into words, but Simone had not shown any convincing signs of relief.

Therapy with Simone

We decided that Simone should receive therapy. I chose to do the therapy in Simone's own familiar surroundings and with Susan at the periphery. We had agreed on the framework, and when I came to the residential section, Simone sat in her highchair at the table, staring blankly into space. She sat at the head of the table, and I took a seat at the side of the table, at about one-and-a-half metre distance. I greeted her and said her name, I introduced myself and mentioned to her that we already knew each other. From the moment I "selected" her and introduced myself, she looked at me with big, serious eyes.

"Susan has told me that you are having a tough time. You are sad. You can't eat, play or sleep. Susan has told me that this time you're wondering if you'll ever see your mother again."

While I was talking, Simone's gaze was intense and serious. I continued,

"Naturally, you get upset when your mother doesn't come to see you, as she normally does. You love her, and she loves you. She will always be in your heart. But suddenly she stayed away!"

My words were accompanied by spontaneous gestures, and when I said the last word, apparently I made a gesture with my hands, because Simone repeated the word "away" while copying my gestures. We looked at a photo of her mother, and for the first time during the therapy session, Simone broke our intense gaze contact, and we both looked at the picture.

"We all understand your longing, how much you miss your mother. Susan knows it, Connie knows it, we all know it. But suddenly mummy stayed away."

This time when I said "away" I turned the photo face down on the table. Simone picked up the picture, looked at it, turned it face down on the table and said, "Away".

"Susan tells me that you don't eat and drink, and that you have trouble sleeping. That can happen when something is really hard to deal with."

At this point, Simone again repeated the "away" gesture.

"But you're not going to bring mummy back by starving yourself. And you can't look out for her by staying awake at night. Hanne [the night watch] looks after you at night, and she wants to help you sleep. You need to eat and drink, so that you'll be alive when mummy comes back. Marianne [social worker] has asked the police to find mummy".

I ended the session by saying goodbye and told her that we would talk again in a couple of days. In the meantime, Susan regularly repeated what I had said. The next day the staff in her group said that Simone showed clear signs of relief. She took more of an interest in the world around her, babbled a little, and a few times she had gone over to the photo of her mother, had looked at it and said "away", accompanied by the characteristic gesture.

In the second therapy session, the setting and the time were exactly the same. We sat in the same seats, and Susan again sat at the periphery of the room. Simone insisted that the photo of her mother was brought over, and we looked at it and talked about mummy and about missing her. Simone kissed the photo, then suddenly changed her expression and slapped the photo while she looked at me. I said,

"It's okay for you to be angry with mummy when she doesn't come to see you. Your angry feelings can't control mummy. We don't know why she has stayed away, but when she returns she can tell us".

After this, I told Simone exactly the same words as in the first therapy session. Her eye contact was intense, and her breathing was shallow and rapid. Again, Susan repeated the words from the therapy sessions several times over the next two days before my third session with Simone. Simone showed convincing signs of improvement. She enjoyed her food and was more cautious and critical in her selection than usual, both in relation to food and drink. Her sleep became increasingly restful, and she was able to sit up in bed and watch Hanne care for the other children. She smiled at Hanne and accepted the juice she was offered and then lay down to sleep.

The third therapy session repeated the content of the two previous ones. Our connection was intense, and our communication unequivocal. I emphasised that Marianne had been in touch with the authorities, and that they had not located her mother. Again, Susan repeated the content of the therapy over the following days.

Two days after the third therapy session and after a total of sixteen days' absence, Simone's mother came to Skodsborg and had a talk with Marianne before she went to see her daughter. Marianne told her how strongly and expressly Simone had displayed her emotions, and what we had done to help her. Marianne prepared the mother to expect Simone's rejection and anger, both as testimony of Simone's love for her and as a sign of the neglect she had experienced.

The mother was rejected by her child, but with support from Marianne, Susan and the other professionals in the section, she was able to rebuild her good relationship with Simone, so convincingly in fact that Simone went to live with her mother one year later.

Therapeutic reflections

Not just the staff in her group but everyone at Skodsborg saw the change in Simone. Apart from the obvious joy over seeing a child pull through a crisis, we were also relieved that Simone did not have to be hospitalised.

In our interdisciplinary team we discussed what had led to Simone's recovery, and we analysed the combination of planned and random circumstances. Apart from the therapy itself, we view the caregiver's role as particularly important. When a child is not thriving, the professional does everything she can to help the child get better. During Simone's crisis, Susan was at work full-time every day to ensure a high degree of continuity for Simone.

In this case, the staff comes to see me (IT), because I am the in-house psychologist. The cry for help is heard, an intervention is planned and initiated. The primary caregiver is involved in both the planning and the intervention and is assigned the key role as co-therapist. It is this partnership that brings about Simone's recovery. In this process, the caregiver's work and responsibility are taken very seriously. She is listened to and shown respect. By coming to the section where the child lives, the psychologist, in a sense, instils a specific professional focus and awareness. Multiple observers follow the process as it unfolds, and the psychologist's words to Simone are heard by others.

At Skodsborg we distinguish between *infant therapy* and the *method that characterises infant therapy* applied in everyday here-and-now situations. Infant therapy is always carried out by a psychologist, but other professionals use the method of infant therapy as part of their everyday work. They are constantly using the technique of putting feelings and incidents into words to support the children.

Caroline Eliacheff says, "The words suffice". Because it is so difficult to imagine words as detached from the other aspects of interpersonal communication, we are critical of the content of this brief statement. In Simone's case, the words are key, but they take on special meaning when they are supplemented by eye contact, tone of voice, modulation, gestures, and mimicry. In this case, a particular hand gesture takes on crucial meaning in our communication. We look at a photo of Simone's mother, and Simone takes an active stance to the photo, displaying feelings of both love and anger.

The words that I prepared for Simone's therapy match what Dolto or Eliacheff would have proposed. I have had the opportunity to discuss a number of issues, including Simone's therapy, with Caroline Eliacheff when I went to see her in Paris to receive supervision. She generously offered her reflections on the therapy courses I described to her. In her assessment, the brief, intense process was essential to Simone, who had a convincing recovery. She added, however, that I might not have needed to ask her to eat. Not to eat is the same as being a baby again. When Simone was hungry, as a baby, her mother would feed her. Thus, when Simone stopped eating, that was her attempt at becoming a baby again and bringing her mother back. Therefore, it would have been important to say to Simone, "Your mother is not here. She has a tough life, with many problems, but that has nothing to do with you. We are looking for her, and we are going to find her". Caroline Eliacheff said that that would have been enough to make Simone start eating again.

Therapy format

In the format we strive for we embrace the aspects that are emphasised by Dolto and Eliacheff, while other aspects are toned down or left out entirely.

I greet Simone in a formal and respectful manner. I mention her name, and I introduce myself. I always introduce myself by my full name. I also tell her that I am a psychologist, and that a psychologist is someone who speaks with children and adults.

Simone sits in her own seat. She is physically distinct and separate from her caregiver, which emphasises that she is an independent person with her own integrity. She is her own person. I position myself at a right angle to Simone to ensure that if Simone looks straight ahead she is not looking at me. I do not wish to demand eye contact from her; on the contrary, I want to give her the opportunity to avoid eye contact if she needs to.

I tell Simone that Susan has told me that she is having a tough time, and then I specify what that involves. I do this to show her the same respect that I would show an adult.

I tell her the truth. I pass on the caregivers' observations, and when I suggest a link between her symptoms and the loss of her mother, I say, "maybe" and "we can't know that". This means that I avoid offering a direct interpretation of her physical symptoms. I suggest the possibility that this may be the way it is, but I do not conclude that the link necessarily exists.

Both Françoise Dolto and Caroline Eliacheff often interpret the meaning of the current physical symptoms and the connection between a specific symptom and a specific trauma. They are both experienced doctors, and in addition to their medical training, they are both psychoanalysts. Perhaps this makes it more legitimate for them to offer these interpretations. However, the range of possible explanations and findings when it comes to the connection between trauma and symptom is so wide that we risk getting it wrong. Therefore, we stick to what we know and what we observe.

I offer hope. That is one of the unwritten rules in all therapy, but in infant therapy the rule is stated explicitly. I tell Simone that she needs to eat and drink so that she will be alive when her mother returns. The word "when" indicates that I expect and take it for granted that her mother will show up and return to see her child. What if the mother dies from an overdose? Would that mean that I had lied to the little girl? No, because I actually do believe that the mother will return, and I offer hope. That gives Simone something to live for. If Simone's mother had passed away, we would have had only one option, which is to engage in a new therapy process with Simone, where I would say, among other things, "I was mistaken".

My therapy with Simone was my first infant therapy experience, and I had been building up to it for some time. I had prepared for what I would do, should the situation arise. The situation arose when Simone suddenly, from one moment to the next, found herself facing a severe crisis. She became detached and was unable to eat or drink. Her liquid intake was so low that we considered having her hospitalised. That was the situation when we considered therapy.

The therapy had a convincing effect. Simone had not been in proper contact with her closest caregivers for three days. When I greet her, introduce myself and say her name she looks at me with an intense gaze. No one can have any doubt about the intense contact that is established between us. But it was puzzling for the two caregivers who observed the therapy from the periphery. They had done everything to accommodate Simone, yet they had failed to establish close contact. I walked in the door and established contact instantly. Dolto explains this phenomenon. To paraphrase her explanation, it is not possible to combine the role of caregiver with that of therapist. Therapy must be performed by a therapist. That is also the case in therapy with infants. Caregivers can speak to the child. They can repeat the words from therapy, with reference to the therapy experience, as they did with Simone, and thus take on the role as co-therapists.

"The case of Simone" had a significant impact at Skodsborg. Everyone had seen what a difficult time Simone was having, and in their concern that she might become dehydrated, they had even begun to consider whether she might need to be hospitalised. However, the effect of the therapy made this unnecessary.

The staff members who had been sceptical of therapy with infants took an interest in the method, and the Danish versions of Dolto's book *Seminaire de psychanalyse d'enfants* (1988; French original 1985) and Caroline Eliacheff's *À corps et à cris, être psychanalyste avec les tout petits* (1994; French original 1993) became required reading for everyone on the staff. Over the following years, the method that characterises infant therapy became an integrated and recognised part of the treatment programme at Skodsborg. At some point in their stay here, all children receive therapy, and the method of the approach is widely used by all the caregivers on a daily basis. Several other residential facilities have been inspired by the work at Skodsborg, and many psychologists and therapists have found inspiration and received supervision here. At some point we became aware of the potential of using this approach with children who had either been put up for adoption or who had already been adopted.

Case: Eric. A child who was put up for anonymous adoption

A social worker from a nearby municipality contacted Skodsborg for assistance about a case concerning a pregnant woman with a chronic mental illness who was considered permanently unfit to care for her child. The authorities were considering mandatory adoption. Her due date was a little more than two weeks away, but a caesarean section had been planned two weeks early, in part due to concerns about the health of the unborn child and in part because her due date was in the middle of a week of national holidays when Child Protective Services would be closed. We accepted the case.

On the day of the scheduled delivery, both the appointed primary caregiver, Beth, and I (IT) were present in the maternity ward, along with the social worker. The child was delivered, and the mother received post-operative care. The social worker went into the delivery room and told the mother about the decision that had been made. Subsequently, Beth went to see the mother who was a bit battered after the procedure. A nurse sat at the head of the mother's bed, with the baby in her arms. Beth was emotionally affected by the situation, intuitively identifying with the mother's situation. Beth introduced herself to the mother with her full name and told her that she would be looking after Eric during the first months of his life, and that she would take good care of him. The baby was handed over to Beth, and they came into the hallway where I was waiting. Together, we were shown to a room in the paediatric ward. Here, Beth and Eric would spend a few days while Eric underwent the necessary health checks and assessments.

When we were alone in the room, I told Eric his own story for the first time, only a few hours into his life. He received infant therapy while Beth held him in her arms, wrapped in his blanket. I told him that he had been born today in this hospital, and that it had been decided that he was not going to be raised by his mother. Instead, two other parents would be found for him, who would raise him. Until they were found Beth would take good care of him.

His mother loved him, and he would always hold her in his heart, just as the mother would hold him in her heart. Eric looked up at me briefly from time to time; otherwise, his eyes were closed. After spending a few hours with them I left the hospital.

The following morning I was contacted by the social worker who had been contacted by the hospital. The mother had requested to see her baby. This was unexpected for the municipal administration, but of course we would help make it possible. We arranged a time for the mother's visit with her son later that day. Beth and I prepared for the meeting. We set up chairs in a circle, one for each. One for Eric's mother, two for Beth and myself, one of us holding Eric, and two for the contact nurses assigned to the mother and child. We wanted to make the situation as pleasant as possible, minimising the mother's stress, and we wanted to preserve the situation in words and photos for Eric's life book and for the mother. I asked the staff to find a little table and something to drink. I took charge, acting as "caravan leader".

When the mother came into the room with her contact nurse I shook hands with both of them and introduced myself. The mother had brought a camera. Once we were all seated in the circle, we told the mother about the events of the previous day, Eric's birthday. Beth talked about Eric, and I briefly outlined the infant therapy approach and what I had told Eric. The mother nodded from time to time, and in this way, Eric heard his story one more time. At this time, Beth asked the mother whether she would like to hold her child. She did. Eric was placed in his mother's arms, facing Beth. Beth told him what was happening: "Now you're in your mother's arms. I am sitting next to your mother". We were silent together, while the mother calmly looked at her child. After a while I asked whether I could take a few photographs, and the mother nodded. I took some photos, using both the mother's camera and my own, and told her that we would have the photos processed quickly and sent to the social worker, who would then pass them on to the mother. After about ten minutes the mother handed Eric back to Beth, who held him so that he faced his mother.

There were two stuffed animals in Eric's cot. I asked the mother about the story, and she told us. I spoke briefly about the importance of transitional objects (see Chapter Nine). I asked her whether there was anything she wanted to tell her child, or whether there was anything that was especially important to her that we needed to pass on to his future adoptive parents. There was not. The mother said goodbye to her child. She had named him Eric.

Therapeutic reflections

A sense of urgency and confusion in a municipal administration, which was further pressed for time because of upcoming holidays, was transformed into a targeted effort with a professional approach. Infant therapy and its method formed a secure framework for the key moments when Eric was separated from his mother and the following day when the mother said goodbye to her child. Thus, Eric's story came off to a good beginning, despite the grave decision by the authorities.

Eric suffered a loss when he was separated from his mother. We are aware of that. Nevertheless, in our intervention we strove to ensure a gentle transition from his life with his mother to his life with Beth. This afforded him the necessary protection and helped minimise the risk factors. The two nurses who, as part of their professional duties, suddenly found themselves in a therapy situation, found the experience fascinating. In a subsequent conversation, they discussed what had made the biggest impression on them, and they both pointed to the calm atmosphere, the silence during those important moments and the support that was provided for both mother and child; factors that are key aspects of the method that characterises therapy with infants.

When a child receives infant therapy, or when the method of infant therapy is used with a mother while others are present, as in the Eric's case, everyone is affected by the content of the therapy and of the ceremonial character of the situation. That is also the case when the method is used with adults. A situation that could easily have been emotionally driven, filled with random occurrences and chitchat, is transformed, by the concept of infant therapy, into a therapeutic experience characterised by a calm, secure atmosphere, to the benefit of all involved.

CHAPTER THREE

Therapy with infants as it is practiced at The Family House in Horsens

The basic therapeutic approach at The Family House

The Family House in the Danish town of Horsens is a psychotherapeutic treatment facility where the target groups are pregnant women with special needs and parents with children aged from nought to two years, whose development is at risk. The purpose of the treatment here is to intervene in the child's life as early as possible to create a safe environment, counteract a negative social legacy, and strengthen the parents' footing in the labour market.

The therapy that is used to effect change in the families deviates from previous psychotherapy approaches, which were more firmly anchored in Freudian thinking and its emphasis on interpretation and on making the unconscious conscious. The work at The Family House is more driven by object relations theory, empathic accessibility, corrected attachment experiences and improving the parents' self-esteem. If a person has been marginalised since childhood due to developmental delays or deficiencies, close, continuous and respectful therapeutic contact can be a source of learning, relief, renewed hope, and a possibility for change that may become a source of strength in the future.

However, when the target group is at-risk parents and their children, it is crucial to pick the right intervention approach.

A theorist who has been especially influential in relation to the approach we have developed at The Family House is Daniel N. Stern (1934–2012), who was a professor of psychology at the University of Geneva. In his book *The Motherhood Constellation* (1995) he writes about the work in the Geneva group and the San Francisco group. In the Geneva group, the clients are parents in well-off families. They mostly represent intact nuclear middle-class families who are seeking therapy on their own initiative. They are capable of retaining their newly acquired knowledge between therapy sessions. That is not the case with the families in the San Francisco group. Here, the clients have typically been referred to therapy because the child's development is at risk. It takes a considerable effort from the therapist to establish a sustainable therapeutic alliance. Stern's message is that at-risk families need a therapeutic approach where the therapists are much more present in the families' everyday life and come to serve as role models for the families.

Psychotherapy with parents and infants, as it is practiced at The Family House, is quite similar to the work that Stern describes with the clients of the San Francisco group. The therapeutic work at The Family House is based on the post-Freudian model of psychoanalysis—a model that is appropriate for the treatment of people with personality disorders and affective disorders, among others. Prior to 1998, day patient psychotherapy was mainly aimed at the parents. The idea was that if the parents thrived, so would the children. It was helpful for the children if the parents learned to master their own lives and see the children as they were.

However, for some children, that was not enough. If the child's energy was stuck in a traumatic experience that the child was unable to contain or let go of, the trauma would stay in the body, disrupting the child's development and causing disorders of varying severity. Since we became aware of the potential of infant therapy in 1998, we have enthusiastically included this approach in our work at The Family House, and together with Inger Thormann we have continued to develop the method that characterises infant therapy. This has opened our eyes to the benefit that even very young children can derive from this therapeutic approach. The sooner the traumatised child receives therapy, the easier it is for the child to recover and move on. Not all the children who visit The Family House receive infant therapy, but we actively consider whether the child would benefit from the approach. This practice of active consideration not only applies to The Family House but also to the Family Service under Horsens Municipality, where the family coun- sellors are aware that children in any family may experience trauma and need infant therapy.

Sometimes, children are referred to The Family House who have given up contact with others and become dispirited. They avoid con- tact. They appear pale and translucent. Some children are limp, while others are constantly tense. A common characteristic is their blank gaze. Even if they look at someone, there is no sense of "meeting", and they seem to be looking right through the person. When an attempt is made to initiate an interaction they may briefly look up without, however, engaging in actual contact. Left on their own, they move around aim- lessly. Physically, they are often very active, have difficulty settling down and have sleep problems. They do not cry like children normally do but often scream in frustration.

These children need predictability and routines, and they need everything to follow a familiar pattern. In the nursery they show no interest in the other children but withdraw to their own space, usually going around by themselves, and typically do not worry about being lost. They contact adults when they need assistance, for example if they want a box of toys that is out of reach. They engage the adult for the specific purpose of getting the box but do not establish actual contact. They briefly rearrange the toys in the box without really examining it. They are often fascinated with moving objects and may, for example, watch with a bemused smile, as the laundry goes around and around in the washing machine or gaze at a piece of string that they slowly pull through their fingers, again and again. Typically, these children hardly ever have somatic illnesses.

Early chaotic experiences

When a young child gives up contact with others and slips into his own world, the need for an intensive intervention is urgent. In infant therapy, we put the child's chaos into words. By seeing the child and putting his experience into words, we can help bring order to the child's chaos; thus, the chaos no longer constitutes a closed system but is an identified part of life.

In our experience, when a child withdraws from contact and abandons all attempts at living in a relationship with others, the cause lies in early chaotic experiences and a lack of coherence that is impossible for the child to escape. It is like a broken record where the needle is stuck in a groove, unable to move on without outside assistance. The therapist has to put the events and the child's reactions into words to enable the child to place the event in context and let it go.

Part of the background for the severe symptoms may be that no one until now has put the disturbing and incoherent experiences into words. This lack of communication hinders the child's ability to relate to others. The child needs to share his experiences with another. When the child's experiences and feelings are neither received nor known by another, the child is stuck in a perceived sense of meaninglessness. The child is at the mercy of his sensations, and when these are not articulated and structured by another person, they turn into peculiar, arbitrary and scary phenomena.

When the child's chaos stems from a trauma, the therapy has to revert to a point in the child's life that offered a basic sense of security and put the good features and qualities into words; next, we proceed to telling the child what happened when the difficulties began.

Infants are quick to regain their sense of security once they receive therapeutic assistance.

Case: Mark

A couple, both thirty years old, are expecting their first child. The delivery is to term, but there are severe complications during the delivery, which takes a very long time. The mother is so worn out afterwards that she is unable to be with her newborn son right after birth. Shortly after birth the boy develops an infection, and the parents are worried about losing their little boy and arrange for an emergency baptism in the hospital. He is given the name Mark. The parents are struggling, but no one sees just how hard this is for them, perhaps because they are both articulate and good at keeping it together. The mother withdraws further. Mark feels his parents' pain and rejection, and he too withdraws. This makes the mother feel that she is failing as a parent, which in turn causes her to withdraw further, and the negative spiral has begun.

The family is released from the maternity ward. They are insecure. The parents have recurring disagreements because they both feel overwhelmed and powerless to deal with the situation. Mark cries often and rejects contact. The father feels defeated and spends more and more time at work. The parents watch Mark retreat further into his own world. They wish to see their boy as a healthy, thriving boy, but they are painfully aware that he is different from other children. Mark and his parents are referred to The Family House when Mark is one year old. At that point, he and his parents have no mutual contact. Mark lives in his own world, and his gaze shows no sign of recognition. He looks at us therapists with a blank stare. He responds only briefly to attempts at contact. He walks aimlessly around the therapy room. The parents tell us that he has significant trouble sleeping, and that they find it difficult to comfort him. Their inability to engage him properly is very painful for them. They feel that they are failing as parents. The lack of emotional response is deadly—not only for the child but also for the parents. Has their relationship been broken, or was it never established? The parents note, with pain, that Mark does not respond to their attempts at engaging him. After the referral to The Family House, the psychotherapist who is assigned to the family visits them at home twice a week for sessions aimed at strengthening the relationship between the parents and Mark. Observations and talks with the parents make it clear that Mark would benefit from infant therapy. Additionally, the parents are offered individual therapy.

Mark, who is now one year and three months old, had a total of six therapy sessions. Each session was carefully planned. In the first session we focused on Mark's start in life, where he was the fruit of his mother's and father's love, a wished-for child, and where the initial time in the mother's womb went well. Each session ended in an explicitly stated hope, for example, "Daddy and mummy know that it has been difficult for you, and they are ready to offer you their help and support". During therapy, Mark sat between his mother and father. He looked briefly at me (IP) when I spoke to him. When it was Mark's bedtime in the evening after the first therapy he insisted that his parents had to sleep in the big bed too, all three of them spooning. The parents were astonished, as Mark had never previously wanted close physical contact.

In the second therapy session I told him about his mother's anxieties about the delivery. About his unpleasant experience of being stuck and about the chaos that surrounded the delivery. The hope that I held out to Mark was that he had a strong will to live, and that he had survived. Mark listened, most of the time gazing away but occasionally looking at me with curiosity. In the days following the second therapy session, Mark began to seek contact with his parents.

In the third therapy session I told him of the parents' profound sense of relief and joy when he was born. Mark listened but with an empty gaze. After the third therapy session, he engaged his parents even more. For a long time, Mark had screamed in frustration when he had his nappy changed. He still screamed, but his screams were now less intense.

In the fourth therapy sessions I told him about the time when he fell ill, about the pain and discomfort of having a tube put through his nose, about being in an incubator, with all the noises and the machinery that helped him breathe. The hope this time was that it was a good thing that the doctors examined him, even though it hurt, because it helped him recover and go home with his parents.

In the fifth therapy session I told him about the chaos that surrounded him, because the adults were worried for his life, his baptism in the hospital, that he might have sensed his parents' anxiety and despair as well as my own thoughts about what it might have been like for him to go through this. Mark listened but still regarded me with an empty gaze with occasional stolen glances. After the fifth therapy session the parents said that it was now much easier for them to put Mark to bed at night, and that his screaming had almost ceased.

In the sixth therapy sessions I told Mark how he improved more and more and eventually recovered so much that his parents could take him home. Mark listened but insisted on moving down on to the floor to a doll's house in the room. I told him about what had happened while he examined the doll's house. At home, Mark continued developing, gradually increasing contact with his parents, and a positive spiral had been set in motion.

When Mark was four years old the family visited The Family House. Mark seemed happy, and he spontaneously talked about his day in preschool. Later, he involved his father in rough-and-tumble play. While they played he made sure that their rough-housing did not get out of hand, lest his father be hurt. He had good interactions with both parents. There is no doubt that they love Mark, and that he knows that they love him. Mark now attends a regular preschool, he is popular, the other kids miss him when he is not there, and they come out to greet him when he arrives in the morning. Mark loves his preschool and thrives better than expected in many areas. In preschool he has three weekly support lessons.

When the parents are part of the infant therapy process

Both the child and the parents (or the caregivers who are in the parents' place) need to take part in infant therapy. The therapy involves the family as a whole. The parents often carry an inner pain related to the traumatic experience which they know that the child had. The parents are often burdened by feelings of guilt and shame. Often, they try to put it behind them; but like the child, they carry the pain in their bodies. Parents often try to reassure themselves by telling themselves that since the child was so young, she had probably forgotten what happened. The child has not forgotten. The body remembers. When the parents try to forget, the child is left alone to face the traumatic experience. Many parents say that the pain has acted as a barrier to contact, and that it is therefore a huge relief, both for the child and for the parents, when the issue is put into words. It is no longer silenced but constitutes a shared pain that is allowed to exist.

In infant therapy, we put the actual event into words after discussing the incident in depth with the parents to enable them to contain the child with her pain. In many cases, the child will hold the parents in a long and intense gaze during therapy, as if to say, "Is that what it was like?" It is the parents or those acting as the child's parents who are the caregivers for the child in this situation.

The therapist is not a caregiver but someone who enters the child's life with a specific therapeutic goal. As the "caravan leader", the therapist has an authentic personal presence in the moment, synchronises with the child and puts the concrete incident into words, while the parents act as witnesses. Afterwards, the therapist leaves the child's life and does not return until it is time for the next therapy session. The therapist gives the parents a written version of the therapy message to enable them to repeat the words to the child.

A family may be referred strictly for infant therapy. In that case, we do not know the child beforehand but gather information by speaking with the parents. In these cases, we tell the child that we are relying on information from the child's parents. If the family is already receiving treatment at The Family House, we observe the child and gather information from the parents and from the case file. We try to learn as much as possible about the child. What is the child telling us with her behaviour? What do we know about the child's past? If we find that infant therapy would be helpful for the child we tell the parents what we observe, and what our thoughts are on the matter. We ask them what they see, and what their thoughts are. What happened, precisely? If they put themselves in their child's place, how does each of them imagine the child perceived the situation?

We tell the parents about infant therapy and give them literature about the approach to take home. If the parents want us to try to ease the child's pain using infant therapy, we prepare for the next meeting by drawing on our professional skills, our knowledge, and our intuition. How do we imagine the infant experienced the specific course of events? What do we need to put into words to help the child? The specific message is written down, and we are happy to lend the child our perspective, for example, "Perhaps you missed mummy!"

Before the therapy begins we meet with the parents and present the session plan. We give the parents a written outline of what we are planning to tell the child. We are very careful never to put the parents down. We ask the parents to consider whether what we are planning to say to the child feels right to them. We prepare the parents and the staff in the child's day care facility that the child may react, for example by being more agitated the first day or so after therapy. This is merely an indication that the child is affected by what we have said, and the child will soon do better than she did before the therapy. We work with the parents to find the right words, until they feel that "that's what it was like". Some parents may need to work on their feelings of grief and guilt. When the parents can handle seeing the therapist deliver the message to an empty chair where they envision the child being seated, everyone is ready for the first therapy session.

The actual therapy process

We make sure that the room is undisturbed. Preferably, the child should sit in his own chair, either in a baby seat or in a high chair. The mother and father are seated within reach of the child. The therapist sits at an angle, so that the child is free to choose whether he wants to look at the therapist or not. As therapists we avoid any physical contact with the child.

The therapist

Before the child arrives the therapist spends about half an hour alone, thinking about the child, putting herself in the child's place and preparing the message. It is crucial that we take our time, that we are authentic and respectful, and that we address the child directly. We listen and activate all of our senses to understand what the child communicates. The therapy session is recorded on video.

After the therapy session

In between the therapy sessions we invite the parents in for follow-up meetings as needed. We like to talk to them about their impressions from the therapy, how the child has reacted at home, and whether there are any observations from the child's nursery/preschool. We may show a clip from the therapy session that highlights reactions we need to discuss. To the parents, it is often a very special experience to watch the video and see how their child listens to the therapist and responds, often wordlessly but with sounds, breathing, and facial mimicry.

Therapeutic experiences

Children who were referred for a severe eating disorder often begin to eat normally, and children who were unable to settle down for the night and fall asleep regain their calm and often begin to sleep at night. In children with insecure attachment we see an emergent attachment behaviour. We see that stressed children who have been able to settle down and relax inside their own skin find their calm and begin to relate to the outside world.

In our experience, infant therapy lets us work with the children in a targeted approach. We see their development improve, and we see them regain their inner strength. Without therapy, many of these children would be stuck in stereotypical experiences that they would be unable to let go of. Their development would be restricted, and they would often require extensive support for the rest of their lives.

Children who have a lot of energy trapped in a trauma are often excluded by the community of their peers before they even finish preschool. Infant therapy lets the parents see life from their child's perspective. They develop a better understanding of the child's situation and see how their child engages with the therapist, who also acts as a role model for the parents in the way that he communicates with the child. Some parents tell us that what used to be a vague pain that dominated their relationship with their child has now been identified and become much less prominent.

Infant therapy is targeted therapy for infants, but in practice it acts as therapy for the whole family.

CHAPTER FOUR

Case: Adam

Background

One day, a municipal social worker called my (IP) private clinic in the Danish town of Jelling, seeking therapeutic assistance for a family with a child who was very ill. The professional team supporting the family was concerned whether the parents would be able to continue to care for the child, who required the parents' care around the clock. The family clearly needed help, but how could they help the family escape the current painful and hopeless situation?

Adam was the family's first-born. He was eleven months old. A few hours after he was born, a nurse happened to notice that his skin had an unnatural blue sheen, and that he seemed very limp. Adam was diagnosed with a heart defect that required emergency surgery. Adam was placed in an incubator and transferred to a different hospital that specialised in infantile heart disease. Here he underwent two surgical procedures. The second operation failed. As a result, Adam spent two months in an incubator. During these two months, Adam was subjected to countless painful examinations and treatment procedures. He received muscle relaxants and painkillers. His future was uncertain.

After two months, Adam was released from hospital, and his parents took him home. The parents said that ever since, Adam had been in a constant state of tension. He was constantly whimpering and seemed tense and tormented. His little body was so exhausted that he would fall asleep from fatigue, only to wake up after an hour. The tense state returned as soon as he was awake. Adam took no interest in the world around him and was most comfortable on his mother's arm.

Adam was hypersensitive and could not handle loud noises or even the sound of voices. Therefore, the family could not have friends over, and their everyday life was completely shaped around Adam's needs. Simple things like opening the mail in front of Adam would trigger a panicky crying fit. His mother recalled the many suction procedures and the countless sterile bags that were ripped open while he was in the incubator. She saw that Adam had developed a fear of the sound of paper tearing. Adam's parents did what they could to support each other, but he insisted on being on his mother's arm.

Since birth and until he was eleven months old and received infant therapy Adam had not been able to have proper bowel movements. On the doctor's advice, his parents fed him mashed prunes and tried medication, but nothing worked, and the parents had to assist him manually, which was a dire burden for both Adam and his parents. The mother was cracking under the strain, both physically and mentally. She lost a lot of weight and was clearly having a personal crisis.

The social worker contacted me based on advice from the family's visiting nurse who had heard about infant therapy. When the parents first visited the clinic they were accompanied by their social worker. I told them about how the French psychoanalyst Françoise Dolto had inspired us to speak to very young children, including infants, and that in my personal conviction, it is extremely helpful for traumatised children when the therapist tells them the specifics of what happened in the situation that triggered the crisis.

Without the parents' cooperation, psychotherapy with young children and infants can be very challenging. It is therefore important to include the parents and help them not to give a traumatic response to the child's anxiety.

If the parents want their child to have therapy after hearing about infant therapy, we encourage them to talk about the child's background and early life: about the pregnancy, about any traumas and illness that occurred, and about situations where mother and child were separated. The concrete events that the parents describe later form the background for the message that becomes the focus of the therapy. Adam's parents described how they had looked forward to the delivery, and how difficult everything became when Adam was born with a heart defect. They described that he had come close to dying several times, and about the complications that occurred. They spoke about their fear of losing him, about the pain, grief and despair, about Adam, who spent two months in the incubator, fighting for his life, and about the difficult time when he finally came home but was unable to be comfortable within his own skin. They spoke about his sleep problems and described how he would finally be so exhausted that he fell asleep but then continued struggling as soon as the most profound fatigue wore off. Adam's parents were worn out and felt utterly alone. Other people had a hard time fully grasping their situation. Eventually, the parents felt that they were losing their grip due to mental and physical exhaustion.

After this contribution from the parents we reviewed what they had told us, but this time we looked at events from Adam's perspective and talked about their ideas about what it had been like for him. Many parents prefer to forget and have found a way to rationalise their own pain. Children carry the trauma in their body, and the body remembers. Consequently, the child is left to his or her own devices when the parents try to forget. Therefore it is important to address the child's experience together with the parents.

For the following meeting with the parents I had outlined a plan for six therapy sessions based on the information they had provided in our first talk. Together, we went over the words I had prepared for Adam. It is essential that the parents feel a sense of "Yes, that's what it was like".

Because Adam's immune system was impaired, and the parents had been told that a common cold might be the last straw for him, we decided to do the therapy sessions in the family home. We arranged to do the therapy at the dinner table in the kitchen and to seat Adam in his high chair. His mother and father would sit on either side of him. They were asked to let him sit on his own, lest they break his concentration by touching him. Adam would reach out to them and seek contact if he needed it. Many parents inadvertently disturb their child during the process because they feel the need to care for their child.

The therapy was recorded on video to enable us to capture Adam's exact expressions later on in order to understand what it tells us. Each therapy sessions contained:

- Identification.
- The story.
- Hope.

The six therapy sessions

First therapy session with Adam, aged eleven months

The therapy always begins at conception. A child who does not know who his or her parents are may give up on life when faced with difficult challenges in life. Therefore we always begin the therapy sessions by speaking about how the child's life began. The parents are always a child's lifeblood. Therefore it is crucial for the child to hear about the birth parents. We never say anything bad about the child's parents but find something that we can acknowledge in them, and which can be a source of pride to the child.

Identification

"Hello, Adam, my name is Inger Poulsen. My job is to speak with children. Your mummy and daddy have asked me to speak with you".

The story

"You were a wished-for child. Your father and mother gave you the gift of life. Your mother carried you under her heart for nine months. Your parents waited for you and loved you. Before you were born your mother had been pregnant with another child. That child died very early, even before it was born".

Hope

"You were strong, Adam, you pulled through. When your mother gave birth to you, and your mummy and daddy saw how beautiful you were they were very happy".

Typically, the child listens to what we say. After the therapy sessions the parents often find that the child responds by being more unsettled than normal for about twenty-four hours, before the child then settles into a more balanced state than the parents have seen so far. After the first therapy session, Adam also responded by being unsettled. He was more whiny and upset during the first hours after therapy. The following day, the family went to visit Adam's grandparents. Here, unlike previous visits, Adam immediately reached out to his grandparents and wanted to sit in their lap. Everyone was astonished to see him initiate contact like that.

Second therapy session

Identification

"Hello, Adam, my name is Inger Poulsen. My job is to speak with children. Your mummy and daddy have asked me to speak with you".

The story

"Your mother gave birth to you in a natural delivery. You were good at drinking milk from your mother's breast. For the first eight hours, everything was fine. Then the doctors discovered that there was a part of your heart that wasn't right. A doctor called Sofie Madsen examined you. I think that the examination must have been unpleasant for you. You were placed in an incubator. It is a warm cot for babies. I think that you must have missed mummy and daddy. You were taken to Skejby Hospital in an ambulance. Mummy and daddy drove there in their own car".

Hope

"You are a strong child, Adam, you made it".
    After the second therapy session, Adam was quite whiny and irritable. Nevertheless, the parents felt that when he was happy it was genuine happiness, in the sense that he was more content, calm, and loving than normal. In situations where Adam had previously whimpered and been unhappy, he was now clearer about what he wanted and what he did not want. Since the previous therapy session, his sleeping

had improved a little. He had only woken up once a night. Once he had slept all the way through the night without waking up. The bedtime routine went much more smoothly now.

Third therapy session

Identification

"Hello, Adam, my name is Inger Poulsen. My job is to speak with children. Your mummy and daddy have asked me to speak with you".

The story

"You know that I am here to talk to you about how difficult it was for you when you were still a baby. Mummy and daddy were so excited to have you. They were sorry that you had such a hard time. You had surgery. You were very sick. You spent two months in an incubator. That is a warm cot for babies. There were many noises. I think that the noises must have been startling to you. The doctors used suction to clear the slime from your throat. I think that must have been unpleasant to you. The doctors decided that mummy and daddy had to leave. I think that you must have missed mummy and daddy. In the hospital, the doctors make the decisions. Your mummy and daddy came to visit. Your mother wanted to comfort you. She reached her hand inside the incubator and caressed you. I think it must have been nice for you to feel that mummy was there. Your daddy bought you a car, a little VW Bubble, as a symbolic gift from your daddy to you that your heart should grow as strong as a VW engine, which can run for many years. You had a pacemaker put into your body. That is a tiny box that helps your heart to keep beating".

Hope

"You had a strong will to live, Adam. You made it, and you got out of the incubator, and mummy and daddy took you home. Even though life was very, very difficult for you, you made it".

After the third therapy session, one month after the first session, Adam slept through the night. The parents began to recover and rebuild their energy. Adam was able to take an interest in things in his environment, and he began to play. Suddenly, his bowel movements became normal, which was a big relief to everyone in the family. For the following four years there have not been any problems with his bowel movements.

Fourth therapy

Identification

"Hello, Adam, my name is Inger Poulsen. My job is to speak with children. Your mummy and daddy have asked me to speak with you".

The story

"You made it out of the incubator. Daddy lay with you in bed. I think that it felt safe for you to have your daddy there. Sometimes your daddy walked around with you on his arm. Daddy and mummy talked about how they would always be there to help you. You had a thrombosis in your leg, and your kidneys had a hard time. I think that it must have been hard for you with all the things the doctors did to your body, and which you couldn't keep them from doing. Adam, with your crying you told them that it wasn't nice, and that you wanted to be left alone and snuggle with mummy. What the doctors did was necessary, Adam. The doctors did what they did to help your body heal and recover".

Hope

"You stood up for yourself, Adam, and you pulled through".

After the fourth therapy session, Adam went through a period where he was very adamant in saying yes and no. This was completely new to the parents. Previously, they had not seen him say either yes or no; instead he had mainly complained monotonously, gripped in pain.

Fifth therapy session

Identification

"Hello, Adam, my name is Inger Poulsen. My job is to speak with children. Your mummy and daddy have asked me to speak with you".

The story

"You were well enough for your mummy and daddy to take you home. When you go to the hospital for a check-up, mummy and daddy see how hard it is for you. You are distressed, and you have trouble eating and sleeping. Daddy and mummy know that the check-ups are necessary. They know that it's hard for you. They want to help you as much as they can. Once, when you were with daddy you were very distressed. You saw that daddy was upset too. It's okay for daddy to be upset too. Even though he is upset, he is going to look after you. Daddy and mummy have noticed that your are startled by the sound of paper tearing. That's a noise that you heard many times while you were in the incubator. The noise came when the nurses opened a package of gloves to clear the slime from your throat and nose. I think that must have been unpleasant for you".

Hope

"You are a strong boy, Adam. You made it, even though it was tough".

After the fifth therapy session, Adam began to reach out to his father. The parents began to believe that Adam could go to day care, which they had never dared hope earlier. During this process I had seen how unsettling it was for the parents every time Adam had to go in for a check-up. Was this the time they would be told that he would not be able to survive? Would he have to go through additional painful examinations? Together, we devised a strategy for the best way for them to help Adam through these examinations. In the future, when they received a letter about another check-up they would summon up their own strength. Since this was the way it was, how could they best help Adam get through it? Inspired by the method used in infant therapy, they decided to give Adam brief and specific information about what the check-up involved and tell him that they would be there for him.

Sixth therapy session

Identification

"Hello, Adam, my name is Inger Poulsen. My job is to speak with children. Your daddy and mummy have asked me to speak with you".

The story

"I have been to your house and told you about the time when you were still a baby. I told you about your heart, which was not well, and how the nurses placed you in an incubator to help you get better, and that you must have missed mummy and daddy. Adam, we are all going to die one day, no one knows when.

The doctors have told your mummy and daddy that you can live for many more years".

Hope

"Adam, you are a strong boy, and you have made it, even though you have been very sick. Adam, daddy and mummy love you, and they are looking after you. That is what I have to tell your today, Adam. Today is the last time I am going to be here to speak with you".

From a little, anxious boy with no appetite for life, we saw how Adam pulled himself together from session to session. In a final conversation with Adam's parents the mother said that she had her life back now, because her son had his life back. The staff at Child and Youth Services in the municipality where the family lived were amazed to see the progress Adam had made in just three months. Previously, Adam only slept when he was so exhausted that his body could not keep going any longer, and even then he only slept for an hour at a time, at any time of day. Now, Adam was easy to put to bed, and he slept through the night. Before, he was tormented around the clock. Now he was thriving so convincingly that he spent several hours in day care every morning. Previously, he was so tense that he was unable to empty his bowels. Now his bowel movements were unproblematic.

After this therapy course, the professionals who had been following Adam and his family wanted to know more about therapy with infants, and we arranged a seminar for eighty-six employees from the municipal Child and Youth Services. Adam's parents also took part in the seminar, where they described their experience with therapy. There was a striking difference between both parents' appearance three months after the therapy ended and their appearance in the video from the final therapy session, where they still bore the marks of the rough time they had been through. The parents had reclaimed their lives. At the seminar, both parents spoke spontaneously and freely, and there was even room for a touch of humour in their story about their hardship.

Now, five years after the therapy, Adam is a happy boy who thrives well. He is in reception class and has a younger brother. The parents sometimes see a deep pensiveness in Adam; a pensiveness that other parents of children who have been close to death also describe in their child.

When a child experiences a trauma, every member of the family is affected. The anxiety and the pain keep all the members of the family in an iron grip. Children are highly sensitive, and they can sense and are affected by the parents' anxiety, which risks undermining the child's fundamental sense of security. In infant therapy as it practiced at The Family House in Horsens, we look out for the whole family but focus on the child. The therapist's structured plan for the therapy sessions signals a sense of direction and hope. The therapy sessions have a reassuringly regular structure where the therapist addresses the child directly. With calm and respectful openness, the therapist synchronises with the child while relating the child's specific story. The parents feel seen, heard, and met in their pain, and it strengthens them and their relationship with the child that they can help to bring order to the child's chaos. Including the parents in the process strengthens the parents' future ability to engage confidently in close interactions with their child—also when the child is experiencing a crisis.

Cleavage in the symbolisation process

In our efforts to determine exactly what is meant by "cleavage in the symbolisation process", we turn to the Jungian analyst Lisbet Myers Zacho, who writes the following :

> The normal secure child will, as he or she grows up, find that he or she is able to maintain a stable inner image (symbol) of the mother's being (scent, voice, breast, hands) that helps the child in the mother's absence.
>
> The traumatised, abandoned child does not experience the mother as a stable feature in his or her life. The child exerts all his or her strength to avoid being dissolved, disintegrated, paralysed in anxious solitude. Therefore the child turns to a cleaved-off image, for example of a dummy, which offers no nourishment, but which

nevertheless is reminiscent of a breast. The dummy is therefore perceived as more reliable, and the child comes to prefer it to the unpredictable breast. The child has cleaved off other images in an attempt to survive. The child who receives infant therapy experiences in this process that the therapist sees the child and is able to help the child understand that he or she is not alone, that someone sees the child and shares the child's pain.

The child hears the words, and we know that children until the age of 9 months comprehend the content/message in any language. Only after this age does the child begin to differentiate. The traumatised child recognises him/herself in the verbal embrace that he or she is held in while being told his or her personal story. Gradually, the cleaved symbolisation process will bring together the respective language tones and develop into healthy and healing symbolisation. Here it serves an important purpose, which is to achieve balance and wholeness in the psychological system—even in an infant. (Zacho, 2001, p. 29) [translated for this edition]

If we compare the description of Adam to the theory of cleavage in the symbolisation process we find that Adam spent the first months of his life in an incubator with noisy machinery and painful procedures. Most of the time he was on his own, without the mother's protective body. He devoted all his strength to avoiding being dissolved, disintegrated, and paralysed in his anxious solitude. A cleavage in the symbolisation process may be a child's only option in the struggle for psychological survival.

CHAPTER FIVE

Affective attunement and special moments

The clinical psychologist Susan Hart was one of the first in Denmark to link developmental psychology and recent neurological studies of emotions, forming a field that she has labelled developmental neuroaffective psychology. Susan Hart is inspired, in part, by modern developmental psychology, where Daniel Stern was a leading figure who is widely known and recognised, also in Denmark, for his seminal books. With regard to recent brain research, Susan Hart was inspired by Antonio Damasio and Joseph LeDoux, among others, and she has drawn on these sources in an effort to link affective brain research with attachment theory and developmental psychology. Later, she has also drawn inspiration from the work of Allan Schore and Peter Fonagy, who are also seeking to integrate recent brain research with psychoanalysis.

Susan Hart has watched the video of Adam's therapy, which is described in Chapter Four, and her comment was, "It's not the words that bring about the release; it is the present moments that are created by the therapist's ability to synchronise with Adam that generate the change"[1].

When the therapist prepares the words to say to the child, he checks with the parents to ensure that the story matches their perception of current and past events and situations. This helps reduce the parents' stress levels. The therapist thus contains both the child and the parents. Throughout, the therapist is well prepared and acts as a responsible "caravan leader". The therapist attunes with the child. Attuning with the child is described by Daniel Stern (2004) as a process which begins with small, ordinary moments that are very brief, natural units in interaction, lasting three to four seconds. To describe regular present moments, Stern uses a metaphor of a bird flitting from branch to branch, where every perching marks a present moment. These present moments may become now moments, which are more emotionally charged, and which stand out because there is more focus on them. These may in turn give rise to moments of meeting, where the ability of the nervous system to intensify and co-regulate with others' activity is increased. These moments of meeting only arise when nervous systems enter into mutual adjustment and self-regulation for both participants. In these moments of meeting, the child's and the therapist's nervous system are linked and there is a mutual awareness where they both recognise the other's experience. In a moment of meeting, attunement is at its most intense, and there is an overwhelming sense of closeness and authenticity. A parental couple has described a moment of meeting in the therapy room as "… a magic moment where everything stood still". It is also this sense of the moment of meeting that new infant therapists describe as such a unique experience.

Daniel Stern's interest in present moments and moments of meeting (the latter a concept that was introduced already in 1995 by the American psychiatrist Louis W. Sander, who was also a member of the Boston group) was inspired by his early (1960–1970) video recordings of interactions between mothers and the infants. Using video technology that was cutting-edge at the time, Stern was able to study the process in slow motion to see the tiniest movements in the mother–infant interactions. This gave him access to a new world, and he saw how the interaction unfolded and began to view these moments as the fundamental building blocks of human experience. In the therapy room, changes also occur as a result of tacit knowledge in the present moment. Stern was fascinated by the wealth of information in tacit knowledge as it is played out in fleeting moments.

Example of tacit knowledge

Mike is picked up from preschool by his mother. Mike looks up at her in a present moment of tacit knowledge to register the quality of his contact with his mother on that particular day. Her voice is a little slurred. Recollected images wash over him, holding a wealth of information stemming from his implicit tacit knowledge that could not be described adequately by explicit verbal means.

By giving the present moment such a central position in psychotherapy, Stern (2004) alters our understanding of how therapeutic change occurs, what matters in therapy, and how our way of being with each other has the capacity to rewrite our past and transform our future. Stern claims that fleeting, emotional meetings beyond language are far more important than the lengthy, deliberate efforts to understand one another on a more conscious level and make meaning by verbal means. Thus, interpretations in the explicit domain are not necessary for bringing about therapeutic change. In fact, it involves a risk that what the therapist says comes to define the agenda at the cost of what really matters to the client.

Example of memory context

One-year-old Adam, who is described in Chapter Four, reacted with panic to the sound of paper being torn. His parents had noticed the same sound in the neonatal unit where Adam spent the first two months of his life in an incubator. Much of the human contact he received occurred when various nurses came over to his incubator, pulled out a pair of disposable gloves and tore the paper seal before inserting a tube into his mouth and throat to clear away slime.

In therapy, Adam listened while the therapist told him what had happened. Several present moments occurred, and eventually he looked up at the therapist in a sustained moment of meeting.

The therapist told him about the gloves and about the chaos that they could tell it triggered in him when the staff tore open the packaging to perform the suction. The therapist spoke about the experiences that occurred now when someone tore open an envelope or tore a page from a newspaper. This reminded him of the opening of the glove packaging and triggered selected fragments from his past. When these fragments are integrated they can help us contain what happens in the present and deal with it without being overwhelmed by anxiety.

The intense, silent contact was concluded when Adam looked up at his mother and then over at his father. The therapist told the parents about the importance of remaining in contact and containing the pain until Adam was ready.

Susan Hart sees that infant therapy contains many present moments where contact is achieved. Often, they feed into moments of meeting with synchronisation between the child and the therapist. To quote Susan Hart:

> The transfer of emotional information is intensified through moments of meeting, and the raised level of energy produces a sense of vitality that promotes the nervous system's emerging capacity for self-regulation and attention control. The moments of meeting are a dyadic expansion of consciousness. … Tiny changes at the right time stimulate the nervous system to reorganize and develop. … When moments of meeting occur in a sequence of mutual regulation, at some point there is a state of relaxation. The regulation and integration of all living systems involves shifts between engagement and disengagement, and the infant needs breaks to be able to self-regulate. (Hart, 2011b, p. 27)

There are indications that when the qualities that are found in healthy parent–child interactions are achieved in the healthy therapist-client contact, the experience generates change, driven by the mutual emotional attunement between client and therapist. When infant therapy works it does so in a balance between attachment and the observance of boundaries. To be oneself in an interaction and to be alone in the other's presence are experiences that exemplify healthy attachment and bonding.

This requires that the therapist has the capacity to synchronise sensory impressions precisely, understands what is going on and knows what sort of disruption in the attachment bond the child has experienced. Where did the attachment bond fail? Meeting and bonding emotionally with the client exactly at the point where the healthy attunement has yet to be re-established serves to regenerate, heal, and build inner experiences and self-regulating behaviour. The key is the attachment experiences that unfold before the content of the words takes on meaning; what we might call a "language before language".

When this process unfolds in the parents' presence the parents become part of the process. They find new ways to attune with their child. The therapeutic work continues in their subsequent contact with child. When the parents repeat what the therapist said to the child, new tracks are formed in the parent–child relationship and in both the parents' and the child's brain/nervous system. That is why repetition is so important. Every time the child receives "the words" the child is seen. It is this experience of being seen that lets us sense our existence, our boundaries, ourselves.

Susan Hart explains that when the neural activation—triggered by external stimuli, for example in infant therapy—does not quite match a previous experience without, however, being too far off the mark, the experience gives rise to a new process or experience. The difference between the new and old experience generates learning or development, which makes the involved neurological circuits more differentiated, stronger, and more connected and causes the experiences to synchronise and integrate. One learns something new while also integrating and synchronising the new experience with one's existing knowledge and experience.

In infant therapy, the therapist's autonomic nervous system speaks to the child's autonomic nervous system. Every time, the therapy proceeds according to the same plan: "I have a song for you"—the voice, the rhythm, the melody. A calm pace and time enough to allow for immersion and breaks are important aspects of the approach. This is where the magic happens. Susan Hart believes that it is in the deep synchronisation with the therapist that the child is able to escape the trauma which the child has no words to describe. Asked whether the words do not matter, Susan Hart responds, "Yes, to the therapist the words are important. The words help the therapist contain the child's experience in a way that lets the therapist be authentic in his or her meeting with the child. If the therapist is not authentic, infant therapy will not be possible"[2].

What is it that makes the therapy effective?

- The systematic and structured character of the situation.
- That there is more at play than just the words.

- That the therapist acts as a convincing "caravan leader"; initially in relation to the parents, which enables the therapist to calm their autonomic nervous systems, and later in the therapy room with the child and the parents.
- That the parents observe the therapist's synchronisation with the child and thus come to see the child in a new light.
- That the therapist's focus is on the child; indirectly, however, the therapist simultaneously works with the relationship between the child and the parents.
- That the therapist is authentic.
- That there is a clearly marked beginning and end to the therapy.
- That the therapist synchronises with the child and is fully attuned.
- That the therapist sets out with tiny micro-interactions—a rhythmic exchange in the sensory system; and that the therapist then addresses the limbic system through empathy.
- That the child is seen and heard.
- That the therapist's autonomic nervous system synchronises with the child's autonomic nervous system.

When the therapist is authentic and meets the child in infant therapy, the child senses the message. The child listens, deep inside. The body remembers. The trauma that has hindered the child's healthy development is dissolved. Being seen and having the traumatic experiences put into words brings order to the child's chaos. Thus, the child's chaos is no longer a closed system but a defined part of life.

This therapeutic approach thus represents a further development of Dolto's method.

Notes

1. A personal conversation with Hart in connection with supervision at The Family House, 2007. Translated for this edition.
2. Ibid.

CHAPTER SIX

Attachment as the foundation of the child's development

John Bowlby

Attachment theory in its current form offers a new and different perspective on the impact of childhood experiences and early relationships on a person's subsequent psychosocial development. The original theory is mainly attributable to John Bowlby (1907–1990), whose original goal was to understand the importance of early attachment and its influence on personality development. He first described the theory in 1969 and continued to refine it until his death in 1990. Many others have been involved in developing attachment theory over the years, either working with Bowlby or in parallel efforts.

The origins of attachment theory

Attachment theory rests on the view of children's psychological development that was held by psychoanalysis in the 1930s and 1940s. John Bowlby was an English child psychiatrist and psychotherapist. The conceptual framework of psychoanalysis was dominated by Freud's stage model, where the child is seen to progress in a linear fashion through an oral, an anal, and a genital stage during the first five years of life. Each stage was distinct from the other stages and characterised by stage-specific behaviour that precisely matched the child's psychosexual development. Crying, seeking comfort, and the physical expression of close emotional relations to the caregiver were seen as behaviours pertaining to the first years of life. Development was expressed in the child's growing independence in a move away from the mother's womb, accompanied by a growing recognition of the father's and society's authority and power.

Bowlby's interest in the role of attachment grew under the influence of his work with delinquent boys who all had had early experiences of "maternal deprivation". He was also interested in typically developing children's reactions to separations from the caregiver, and he saw children's grief over separations as a clear contradiction of the psychoanalytic claim that the child's love of the caregiver was motivated by the need for nourishment.

Attachment is the driving force of development, and the basis for this is found in ethology, the study of animal behaviour. Bowlby pointed out that attachment in newborn children emerges in relation to a person who is able to offer protection and security, not someone who is merely able to provide food. Bowlby documented that emotional bonds between mother and child may develop *without* food as the intermediary. This was a very important finding in the climate at the time, where Freud and psychoanalysis regarded food as the primary need, while the personal and emotional relationship between child and caregiver was viewed as secondary.

Attachment is more than a relationship or a behaviour. Bowlby (1969) defined attachment as attachment behaviour, which includes all the behaviours, in animals and humans, that seek to achieve or maintain physical proximity to another individual who is seen as more capable in dealing with the world. Someone stronger and wiser. It is in this context of survival needs that we should see attachment behaviour.

The definition is largely the same today, almost fifty years later, and among the many contemporary definitions of attachment, we will highlight the following: "Attachment describes an inclination to establish close emotional bonds to certain individuals who are able to offer protection, comfort, and calm; this inclination is present in the infant as an innate property" (Hart & Schwartz, 2008, p. 72) [translated for this edition].

A key point in Bowlby's theory is that human beings have a system of attachment behaviour that is always "on", in the sense that the child will *always* register the caregiver's physical position. When the child feels at risk, either from a perceived threat or because the caregiver is absent, the system of attachment behaviour is activated. The child will display a behaviour that is intended to urge the caregiver to provide care. Attachment behaviour includes actions like crying, reaching out with one's arms and later crawling or walking over to the caregiver. This behaviour ceases when the child has achieved physical proximity to the object it perceives as capable of providing protection from the perceived threat. Attachment behaviour is most prominent when the child is insecure, scared, tired or sick, and less prominent when the child is well-rested and at ease in the situation. The system is never "off" but becomes less visible after the age of three years.

Bowlby found it important to distinguish between (1) attachment behaviour that changes over the course of psychological development and (2) attachment as an intrapsychological state that defines our emotional relations with others. He saw the child's development of attachment behaviour and its cognitive integration in the form of "internal working models" as a fundamental contribution to the later emerging capacity for building emotional relations. This added a new dimension to separation or threats of separation from the caregiver. Children's almost psychopathological reactions to separation from the mother could now be explained within a model that revolved around interpersonal relations. The key role of attachment in personality development was further underpinned by René Spitz's research (1965) into the deprivation syndrome found in children who had grown up in orphanages.

Attachment theory breaks with Freud's stage theory about psychosexual development, as Bowlby saw the satisfaction and frustration of attachment as the determining factors in the child's subsequent ability to build and maintain relationships with others. Bowlby saw the capacity to form relationships as the primary factor of mental health. This view shifts the emphasis from intrapsychological conflicts to interpersonal relations.

Attachment in normal development

John Bowlby's collaboration with the Canadian psychologist Mary Ainsworth (1913–1999) resulted in several theories about attachment. These theories are characterised by two main components. One is the normative aspect, that is, the commonalities in terms of attachment patterns and developmental stages. The other is the individual differences that represent deviations from the most typical patterns.

Although children do not establish attachment to the main caregivers until the second half of their first year of life, newborn children are receptive to social stimulation. Just days after birth, children prefer the mother's voice over the voice of some other woman. Newborn children also seem to recognise the mother's scent. How early the child is able to recognise the mother's face based solely on visual stimulation is somewhat uncertain. Research findings (Pascalis, de Schonen, Morton, Deruelle & Fabre-Grenet, 1995) suggest that the newborn child looks at the hairline and the outline of the face. Thus, children who are just a few days old can be said to possess a rudimentary capacity for recognising the mother's face. Only after about eight weeks is the child able to recognise the mother based on features inside the outer contours of the face. The ability of newborn children to recognise their mother is of course not proof of any mutual emotional bond; however, the recognition reactions do form part of the basis for our ability to engage in interpersonal interactions.

Another, later precursor of actual attachment emerges when children are able to participate in sustained interactions with adults by means of facial mimicry, vocalisation, turning of the head, and arm movements. From around the age of two months, children are not only capable of directing their attention at the adult but also of noticing which emotional message is being conveyed. From this stage forward, the interaction with a dedicated caregiver enables a form of contact and a degree of emotional depth that cannot be achieved with another, well-intended adult. At this stage, which stretches from the age of two to three months until around seven months, children show a higher degree of differentiation in terms of whom they react to emotionally. They begin to distinguish between family members and strangers; they show a preference for certain individuals, and attachment behaviour can be triggered or dampened by certain individuals.

Although children aged four to five months appear to have some degree of preference for a familiar caregiver, we cannot conclude on this basis that children develop actual attachment at this early stage. At this age level, *out of sight* still means *out of mind*. The child is not yet able, for example, to think about the mother when she is not present. The child recognises her and responds to her presence with a joy that is not displayed in relation to strangers but has yet to develop a permanent emotional bond to any one person in particular. At this age, the replacement of the primary caregiver by an adoptive or foster mother is still possible without resulting in a major breakdown in the child's social and emotional life.

Signs of clear-cut attachment

When the child is around seven months old, certain key changes occur. Studies have documented that from this age, it is harder for children to adjust to new places or persons, for example in connection with hospitalisation, foster care, or adoption. From this stage, children display so-called separation anxiety, which includes protest, despair, and detachment, followed by intensified attachment behaviour. The child has reached the actual attachment stage; at this stage, separation reactions, initiatives to seek proximity, and other behaviours demonstrate that the child prefers one or a few specific caregivers.

The clear-cut attachment stage begins around the age of seven months. At this age level, children show an active form of *goal-corrected effort to maintain proximity* to a particular caregiver. The child's attachment behaviour now includes signals such as smiling, crying, and reaching out as well as certain movements, for example following or approaching the caregiver, *clingy* behaviour or *protesting* separation. The child begins to understand that the caregiver continues to exist even when she is out of sight (object constancy). This development of attachment does not mean that the child seeks proximity or contact with the caregiver constantly. There is a dynamic equilibrium between attachment and exploration. How much proximity and contact the child seeks varies with the situation and the child's state. When a child feels secure he focuses on playing or exploring the surroundings and only occasionally checks where the *secure base* is to be found. If, however, a perceived threat occurs, the child is likely to seek contact with the attachment figure.

Goal-corrected partnership

At some point during the first half of the third year of life, another key change occurs in children's attachment relationship. While children aged twelve to twenty-four months relate to what the caregiver does and may try to intervene with her behaviour directly, older children develop an understanding that adults may have feelings and plans that are different from their own. A two-and-a-half-year-old child's cognitive and language development is advanced enough that the child can negotiate with the parents and make plans with them to reach a shared goal. At this age, the child has also developed better impulse inhibition. This means that the plans to reach a certain goal can become more complicated. Now, the child is able to consider what the adult is likely to do before initiating her own action sequence. This means that the child is now able to incorporate the adult's plan as an element in her own plan. The child is also able to inhibit attachment behaviour until the conditions are more appropriate and suit both the child and the adult. This makes it possible to engage in a partnership. A goal-corrected partnership means a *sustained relationship between two individuals—characterised by the mutual adjustment of plans and goals*. As children grow older, they begin to cooperate with their attachment figures to find appropriate priorities for shared plans and goals, which leads to cooperation, a coordination of the control over relationship behaviour.

In an experimental study of the transition to clear-cut attachment and a goal-corrected partnership, Marvin (1977) developed a simple method for assessing children's capacity for inhibiting their goal-directed behaviour and include the attachment figure's concerns in their own plans. The experiment was carried out in the child's home and was recorded on video. The mother showed the child a biscuit and told the child that he could have the biscuit once she had finished writing a letter. She then placed the biscuit where it was visible to the child but out of reach and proceeded to sit down and attempt to write for three minutes. When she was done she gave the child the biscuit. Marvin found that most three- to four-year-olds accepted the situation without much difficulty. However, hardly any two-year-olds were able to accept the mother's plan and wait to have the biscuit. Most of the youngest participants cried, tried to grab the biscuit, pushed the mother's hand away from the paper, grabbed the pen or showed similar signs of uncooperative behaviour (Smith, 2002).

Although three-year-old children are able to incorporate the adults' plans into their own behaviour strategy they are not yet able to imagine that adults' plans exist as mental states. A two-and-a-half-year-old child, for example, may accept waiting while his baby sister has her nappy changed before they can all go to the playground but is incapable of imagining that the mother may have a completely different plan in mind. To understand that the attachment figure has different plans and goals than the child, the child first needs to develop a capacity for empathy that goes beyond his cognitive egocentricity. Around the age of four years, children begin to be able to understand that others may have something in mind that differs from the child's own thoughts and goals.

In 1978, Mary Ainsworth developed the "Strange Situation Test" (SST) to study attachment patterns and individual variations in children aged one to two years. She found that children at this age mainly displayed the following attachment styles: secure attachment, avoidant-insecure, resistant-insecure and the later added category of disorganised/disoriented. The conclusion to the study was that the infant incorporates an attachment pattern or a working model that constitutes the child's individual model of the world that the child refers to when engaging in interactions with others (Thormann, 2009).

Are the effects of negative early experiences irreversible?

Mary Ainsworth's research was followed up and expanded by other researchers, who found that the attachment patterns that had been found in connection with SST in twelve-month-old infants were stable over time. There is widespread consensus that everything that children experience during their first year of life is likely to have a permanent impact.

The assumption that early experiences have a greater influence on our personality development than later experiences is based on the notion of infants as highly malleable beings who will be permanently marked by their experiences, for good or bad. The younger the child, the more receptive, especially in relation to bad experiences. This perception is only true with certain modifications. There is plenty of documentation, and Rudolf Schaffer (1996) concludes that "adverse effects ... need not be permanent but can be reversed under certain conditions" (Schaffer, 1996, p. 395). These conditions, first of all, include *therapy*. We have previously seen how children have not permanently lost their capacity for establishing attachments to others, even if they have been deprived of parental care during their first years of life. Similarly, disruptions in already established bonds with the parents, for example due to separation, also need not have permanent consequences for young children. Experiences of deprivation, neglect, and abuse need not, per se, constitute a permanent impairment merely because they occurred at an early time in the child's life.

Research offers several striking examples. Children who had been placed in extremely under-stimulating institutions from birth developed early retardation that was so pronounced that they functioned at the same level as children who were half their age. Those of the children who were later placed in a different and much more stimulating institution or who were adopted by normally functioning families, however, were able to overcome their early experiences and achieve normal functioning.

At Skodsborg Treatment Centre for Infants (Skodsborg) we have carried out tests and follow-up studies of children who have been placed here after early neglect; these studies confirm Schaffer's conclusions. The studies *Børn i krise* (Children in crisis; Thormann, Boesen & Nielsen, 1990), *Med hjerte og forstand* (With heart and mind; Thormann & Guldberg, 2003) and *Medfødte Alkoholskader* (Foetal alcohol syndrome; Thormann, 2006) suggest that children who receive the help they need often thrive well.

Our experiences concern children who came to Skodsborg at the age of nought to six years. Some of them came to us straight from the maternity ward, while others were referred when the authorities became aware of the neglect they had suffered and took action. We have found that children aged five to six years who have suffered severe neglect have recovered after coming to Skodsborg and finding a refuge where they could settle down, find themselves and gradually feel confident about their own potentials. When these children's need for a wide range of care and support measures, including treatment and protection, is allowed to guide the decision about where the child should live after his or her stay at Skodsborg, the outcome is generally quite good. The Family House in Horsens also has countless examples of children with severe early childhood traumas who have received treatment, including infant therapy, and subsequently found their footing in life, continued their development, and shown convincing progress. The Family House also has extensive documentation for the use of psychoanalysis with children and families (Thornsohn, 2007).

Regardless how dreadful the early experiences may be, they do not trap the person for life. The final outcome is not only determined by what happened but also by subsequent events. That is why seemingly identical experiences can lead to such different consequences for different individuals. To view the early years as a critical period, that is, a time when children are so vulnerable that they will be permanently damaged regardless what happens later in life, is dangerous for two reasons: First, because it may lead to a defeatist view of the chances of helping children who have had bad experiences early in life, and second, because it may give the erroneous impression that older children are not vulnerable.

There is no doubt that there has been a tendency to underestimate children's ability to recover from adverse experiences. Based on the research mentioned above and on resilience studies (Thormann, 2009), it is now clear that all is not lost, even if the early years have been inadequate, and that children have an impressive capacity for developing resilience and recovering. There are indications to suggest, however, that adverse effects become harder to overcome with age. But we should never conclude that it is too late to make an attempt. After practicing infant therapy for more than ten years, we both have increased optimism about the prospects of helping traumatised children and infants.

Internal working models

According to Bowlby's theory (1969), attachment should be viewed as a *goal-corrected control system*. As mentioned earlier, the attachment system organises during the second half of the first year of life. Many of the components, however, are already in place before the age of six months. The newborn baby's crying, for example, sends a signal to the caregiver that causes him to act in a way that increases the chance of proximity to or contact with the infant.

The concept of *attachment*, which is addressed here, is based on the assumption that the attachment figure provides a secure base, and that the regulation of the physical distance between the child and the caregiver plays the most important role. However, Bowlby's ambition went beyond the development of a theory about the regulation of the physical distance between child and caregiver. He sought to develop a general theory about personality development and therefore needed to apply a broader perspective. The concept of working models paved the way for a theoretical expansion that included the child's *inner world*. The models develop in the interaction process between child and caregivers and are shaped by the emotional contact and the quality of the attachment.

The information that is internalised in these models will be based on mutual affirmation and become generalised models that become integrated aspects of the child's personality.

A child who perceives her mother as sensitive, attentive, and caring will construct a model of her as reliable and lovable and thus develop a secure attachment to her, which is extended to apply to other close and significant persons in the child's life. In extension of this positive experience the child is able to develop a model for herself as competent, loved, and respected. On the other hand, a child who experiences an ambivalent and unpredictable mother is likely to construct a model of insecurity in relation to the attachment figure and other close and significant persons and, by extension, to perceive herself as incompetent and unloved. Children's experiences with their caregiver thus shape both their perception of attachment to other close and significant individuals and their self-perception.

As children's cognitive capacity grows they are increasingly able to predict the possibility of a wide variety of situations, including situations that they know will be frightening. No situation that a child is able to predict, according to Bowlby (1973), is more frightening than the thought that the attachment figure will be absent or inaccessible when the child wants contact, and hence, the child develops the strategies reflected by the avoidant, resistant, and disorganised patterns, which serve to protect the child from anxiety. The child needs the attachment figure to be accessible and willing to offer comfort and protection. Thus, accessibility involves both the child's ability to contact the attachment figure and the attachment figure's receptiveness to the child's needs.

Bowlby based his theory about internal working models on three key assumptions:

1. A child who is certain that the attachment figure will be accessible when the child wants contact will be less disposed for acute or chronic fear than a child who for some reason lacks this sense of security.
2. In the course of childhood, the child develops a secure image of the attachment figure as accessible or an insecure image of the attachment figure as inaccessible. These expectations of the attachment figure's accessibility will remain relatively stable throughout the child's adult life.

3. The expectations of how easy or how hard it is to make contact with the attachment figure and of the attachment figure's receptiveness are shaped by real-life interaction experiences with the person.

The development of internal working models

Bowlby did not, however, view the internal working models as rigid and immutable. The models are *mental representations*, which are updated in a natural, developmental process, as the child grows older. This development takes place in connection with the emergence of various cognitive systems at different age levels (cf. Thompson, 1999):

1. Children's social expectations of attachment figures and other familiar persons, which begin to develop during the *first year of life* but are later modified.
2. Representations of more general attachment experiences, which are stored in the long-term memory from the *second year of life*.
3. Auto-biographical memories, where certain events are placed into a personal context from the *third year of life*.
4. The understanding that others have mental states that may differ from one's own—a capacity for empathy or "theory of mind", which emerges some time *between the second and third year of life*.

The first mental representations, that is, the ones that concern the child's relationship with the parents, and which go into shaping a secure or insecure attachment pattern, are assumed to consist of simple social expectations of the caregivers' receptiveness. These working models, which are normally established during the first year of life, form the basis for the cognitively more complex representations of self and interpersonal relationships that develop later.

The early working models are primitive and hence open to modification. Because the working models are constantly revised and updated, the impact of the child's attachment experiences will depend on the degree of security that characterises the working model that is under construction at the given age level. The age of three to four years, for example, is an important period for the development of the self. Secure attachment at this age level may play a greater role for continuity in relation to later psychosocial functioning than secure attachment at the age of one year.

Children's memories of the first auto-biographical events in connection with the self and the relationship with the attachment figures constitute a sort of *shared memory* that is formed in dialogue with important caregivers. By retelling and interpreting key events in the child's life, the caregivers can influence the child's perception of events, and through conversations they can influence the child's emotional reactions and self-perception. With growing cognitive capacity children develop the ability to internalise the interpretations of interpersonal experiences that they have previously encountered in interactions with adults.

Bowlby realised that we need to understand internal working models in a developmental framework. When a child is two to three years old, the models do not yet represent a stable mental state that forms a basis for continuity in the child's development, unaffected by life changes. A more stable model requires a longer development process where multiple factors have the potential to affect what lies between the initial, primitive working models and a more mature psychosocial functioning. Bowlby stands as the pioneer of attachment theory. He carried out a large number of research projects and developed many important theories. Here, we have only addressed the most relevant in relation to the theme of the book: infant therapy. The first scientific studies of children's attachment were carried out in the 1940s. Only after Bowlby's first publications about attachment in the 1950s and 1960s did psychologists and psychiatrists begin to perform direct observation studies of attachment behaviour in infants and young children.

CHAPTER SEVEN

Attachment and separation: abandonment syndrome

As a clinician, Bowlby had taken an interest in the impact of the separation of parents and children even before World War Two (Bowlby, 1940). Later he turned to observations in connection with separation that called for an explanation. One of the first observation studies was carried out in England and included children under four years of age who had been separated from their parents due to the events of World War Two. The second series of studies, which violated basic ethical guidelines by today's standards, involved children who had accompanied their mothers to prison during their first year of life. Initially, they were looked after by their mothers, but later they were separated from their mother for three months and cared for by another mother in the same prison. The separation did not involve any change in environment, apart from the separation from the mother. A third series of studies dealt with situations where either the child or the mother was hospitalised. Despite certain differences in background conditions, the results of these studies all pointed in the same direction: From the age of six months, children show a characteristic response when they are separated from their primary caregiver.

A child who has lost his attachment figure will do everything possible to get her back. This behaviour suggests that the child expects the attachment figure to return; in the meantime, the child typically rejects other people's attempts at comforting the child. The state was labelled *separation syndrome* or *abandonment syndrome*, and Bowlby described it as involving three stages: *protest, despair,* and *temporary detachment*.

Protest and despair

The child's initial response to separation is *protest*. This may last anything from a few hours to a week or even longer. The child seems profoundly distressed by the loss.

Next comes *despair*. This behaviour suggests a growing degree of hopelessness, although there are indications that the child continues to focus on the missing caregiver. The child is introvert and appears to be grieving. The child withdraws from other people and from activities and often sits in her bed with an empty gaze, hugging a teddy bear or another object that the attachment figure has left behind. Bowlby interpreted this reaction as a sign that the child had begun to grieve over the missing caregiver and had given up hope of her return. He felt that adults often misinterpreted the child's apparent calm and inactivity as signs of a positive adjustment, when in fact it was a serious sign of the degree of the child's suffering. The child's postures and emotions could be described with the terms hopelessness, withdrawal and grief.

In the despair stage, the child eats little or nothing and risks substantial weight loss unless he is reunited with the attachment figure or begins to reorient towards the world.

Temporary detachment

Stage three in the separation response, as Bowlby described it, involves *temporary detachment*. *Detachment* is often erroneously viewed as an improvement in the child's condition. The child begins to take more of an interest in her surroundings, no longer rejects the new caregivers and may even smile and engage in social interactions. If the attachment figure comes to visit he or she may be met with an aloof response or even rejection. If the stay at the new location is extended, or if the child is moved again she will eventually act as if loving care is of no importance. This would constitute *permanent detachment*. This stage involves a painful inner drama for the child. On the one hand, the child is grieving, and on the other hand he has left many emotions behind; emotions that are much too difficult for a young child to handle constructively.

Bowlby viewed the child's reactions as a *psychological defence mechanism*. To a casual observer the child seemed not to recognise the mother, indicating that the child had "forgotten" her and therefore naturally treated her as a stranger. Bowlby was convinced, however, that the child's behaviour was not an indication that she had forgotten the caregiver. He argued that in order to survive the extended separation from the mother, the child "shut down" the most painful emotions. Instead, the child focused on retaining a positive image of the attachment figure and on being able to begin to relate to those persons in the environment who were able to offer food, opportunities for play, and other vital contact. The child becomes more focused on himself and on physical objects such as toys, food, and sweets. In this state, the child does not care whether the new caregivers are coming or going, and the child stops displaying emotions to the original caregiver if he or she visits. This is a very serious condition. Studies from the 1940s by Goldfarb, Skeels, and Spitz found that the experience often results in delayed development and atypical social and emotional behaviour, even, in the worst case, psychopathy.

In the framework of attachment theory, detachment represents the young child's immature attempts at putting the attachment system "on standby", since the most important person in the world, from the child's point of view, has become unavailable. Thus, detachment should be seen as the child's endeavour to disconnect the attachment to the adult. If a reunion takes place, the caregiver is put to the test. After a period of meeting the caregiver with a "neutral" attitude the child will begin to relate to the attachment figure based on this experience of abandonment; at this stage, the child will be overwhelmed by pent-up emotions, and the mother will have to accept and attempt to contain the child's full emotional register.

Follow-up studies of children who have undergone similar separations as infants found that in addition to the duration of the separation, the parents' willingness and ability to contain the child's difficult emotions have a significant impact on the child's ability to deal with close emotional relationships later in life (Heinicke & Westheimer, 1966).

The case story below illustrates an infant's emotional struggles after being abandoned repeatedly; it also illustrates that adequate care along with targeted therapy can reduce the negative influence of abandonment on the child's personality development.

Case: Maria

Maria was just over one and half years old when she came to Skodsborg late one evening. She was accompanied by two government officials from another Nordic country. That same day she had been separated from the parents who three months earlier had picked her up from a South American country with a view to adoption. She was referred to Skodsborg as an emergency case. When the request came in, we had emphasised the importance of a few "protective measures". We underscored the importance of saying proper goodbyes, and that girl should be given her most essential belongings with her, including her clothes and toys and any photographs from her life.

The educator who had been appointed her main caregiver at Skodsborg met Maria and the adults accompanying her at the airport, and at Skodsborg we were ready to welcome her with food and something to drink. The caregiver helped Maria settle in, found some of her toys and was there for her. I (IT) tried to uncover a sliver of Maria's story from the officials. My goal was to be able to perform the first therapy session that same night. I had very little information to work with but enough to be able to put together "the words". I briefed our guests on our approach and what I intended to do "in the middle of her arrival". I asked the caregiver to place Maria on a chair on her own with her teddy bear and dummy within reach. I introduced myself to her, told her the name of the place and explained that it was a place for children, a children's home, and that she would be living here for a while. This was something the authorities had decided.

"We know that today you said goodbye to mummy and daddy whom you lived with for three months, and where you thought you were going to stay. But it has been decided that that's not the way it's going to be. We know that you were picked up by these people, who are strangers to you. We know that this is hard for you, and that you must be wondering what's going on. It is always hard to be separated from the people we love. You have suffered many losses, and you are on your own. We want to help you as best we can. We want to help you remember what has happened in your life".

I took the picture of the intended adoptive parents and Maria from when they picked her up in South America and placed it on the table. Maria recognised her teddy bear in the photo and indicated that that was the bear she was holding now.

"It's so nice that you have your bear, and it's nice that we have these photos. They are going to help you remember what has happened in your life".

Before I left Skodsborg that night I typed up the words, so that the caregiver could repeat them to Maria if she felt it was necessary.

On the trip to Denmark, the adults travelling with Maria had repeatedly attempted to put her on their lap, but she had very clearly requested her own seat. She had been quiet, had paid attention to what was happening, had accepted a little food and something to drink. At the airport she was delighted when she spotted her little plastic scooter on the baggage carousel. After arriving at Skodsborg, she was pleased to see her own belongings, and while we adults exchanged information she went around the table on her scooter.

Maria was physically restless. Her facial expression was neutral. When she was picked up and put in a chair she wanted to climb down again but stayed in her seat when she spotted some bread, fruit, and fruit juice on the table. It was in this situation that I initiated the therapy. At first, I spoke her name and said that there was something important I wanted to tell her. She looked at me, looked away, then re-established contact, and I never once doubted that she was paying attention. The caregiver stayed with Maria at night, sleeping in the same room as her to offer the best possible protection in case she woke up at night and needed her presence. But Maria slept well, in her own nightwear and with her teddy bear in her arms.

The following days, Maria was very sad. She would sit still, staring out in front of her, or she would approach an adult and climb up on her lap. She always had the teddy bear with her, and when she was sucking her dummy she slipped out of contact. Maria was in therapy about every other day. During the first week she cried during the sessions. She did not let go of her adult caregiver and demanded to sit on her lap during therapy. We used the photograph of her adoptive parents, Maria, and the teddy bear, and already the first day after her late-night arrival her eyes overflowed, leaving two wet trails on her cheeks. No sobbing, no sound whatsoever, just her eyes overflowing. Maria was clearly in mourning. She had clearly developed an attachment.

A few months old, Maria had been discovered in a market square and taken to an orphanage. Later, she had been transferred to a different orphanage, then picked up once, before she was picked up again and taken to Skodsborg.

Throughout her stay at Skodsborg, the content of the therapy revolved around the same topics: her story and the many separations from caregivers, which might have made her doubt whether there were a mother and a father waiting for her anywhere. But there were, and we assured her of that. We wanted to allow her to grieve deeply and with passion, and we wanted to use our words, in combination with comprehensive care, to help her keep her own story open and engage socially with the children at Skodsborg but also to preserve her faith in a future where there were a mother and a father waiting for her, a family where she could stay for good.

After two weeks at Skodsborg, Maria showed a degree of confidence in the environment that made it possible to conduct the therapy sessions in the therapy room, with her primary caregiver present and with Maria seated on her own little chair. Concurrent with this, Maria began to "run away" from her caregiver, both in the house and in the garden. We discussed how best to interpret her "running away". Françoise Dolto was convinced that a young child who has been separated from his or her parents and who repeatedly runs away is simply looking for the parents. That made sense to us. We decided to intensify our care for her to prevent her from distancing herself from her caregiver by having her follow Maria closely at all times, staying close without invading her space. After this intervention had been in place for two months, Maria surrendered to her primary caregiver. She allowed herself to be drawn in, and an attachment process unfolded right in front of our eyes.

During the now weekly therapy sessions I continued to tell Maria her story. For two months I would put the family photo on the table every time, and we would look at it together. One day I told her that I had decided to put it away. Maria did not object, and subsequently we emphasised the part of her story where she was with her birth mother in her original home country. We spoke of the mother who would always be in her heart, and about the country and the culture that would always be hers. Just as she would always hold her birth mother in her heart, the mother would also always hold her, Maria, in her heart. That the mother had decided that they could not live together did not mean that she did not love Maria. Each session ended with the hope: "There is a mummy and a daddy waiting for you".

Maria's newly established attachment to her primary caregiver, Rita, was to be put to a challenging test, because Rita was going on a vacation that could not be cancelled. Her secondary caregiver, someone whom Maria also had an attachment to, took over the close care for Maria. Rita put together a little book for Maria, using pictures to tell the story of her trip. First, the aeroplane would fly to the country where Rita was taking her vacation, and on the last page it returned to Denmark. The return trip was especially important to Maria. During her short life, she had made two one-way trips, so in her mind, anything could happen. When she was in the garden she looked up when planes went overhead, and several times each day, her caregiver reminded her of the final picture in the book, which showed her beloved caregiver returning home. As she did in fact.

Coinciding with this important experience, Maria was introduced to her new family: her mother, father, and big sister. The meeting between Maria and the family took place as an extension to the infant therapy. I (IT) sat at the head of big table in the living room at Skodsborg with Maria to my right. Next to Maria sat her primary caregiver, Rita, and to my left, facing Maria, sat her new family.

"Now the big day has arrived", I said, addressing Maria directly. "Sometimes you have shown us that you weren't quite sure if you dared to believe what I told you. Many times in your life you have lost people you cared for. But I have told you that there is a mummy and a daddy waiting for you, and there is also a big sister, and here they are".

When I made the introductions, Maria looked, first at the mother, then at her big sister, then at the father. They had brought along photos of the family, and we looked at the photos, one by one, carefully, to give Maria time to understand what was going on.

"Look, here's a photo of mummy. She's sitting here. Here is the photo of your big sister. She's sitting there. And here is the picture of daddy, who's sitting there. In the coming days you will get to know them. It takes a long time to get to know new people".

The transition took place over a ten-day period where they spent time together daily. At first, the family came to Skodsborg, and later there were visits in the family home. Half-way through the transition, Rita came to see me. She said that Maria was "just impossible today". She had never seen her like that before. Maria was acting up on the changing table, making it impossible for either Rita or the new mother to change her nappy. We decided to do a little infant therapy session in the play room. Maria sat in her high chair, and her mother, Rita and I sat around the table.

"Rita tells me that you are squirming so much on the changing table that mummy or Rita cannot change your nappy. There can be many reasons for that. But I think that you're testing mummy. You want to be absolutely sure that she is able to handle you, even when you make things difficult for her. But she is; otherwise she would not have become your mother".

Maria was then carried out to the changing table, where she calmly allowed herself to be laid down and have her nappy changed.

When it was time for Maria to leave Skodsborg we gathered around the table in the play room again, and once again I verbalised what was happening, and what had happened. Maria showed her familiarity with the method of infant therapy as it is practised at Skodsborg, as a good friend and a staff to lean on when coming to terms with the big issues in life.

Therapeutic reflections

Maria had seen several close contacts with others suddenly disrupted. At one point she lost her mother and was entrusted to caregivers at a local orphanage in her home country in South America. Later she was placed in another orphanage, and finally she was picked up by her new parents, who brought her to their home country. After three months, a new decision required Maria to uproot again and be entrusted to new caregivers.

We observed that Maria responded emotionally. She mourned, she showed her feelings, she sought closeness and cried, and she showed that she was fond of her "transitional objects": her teddy bear, her toys, and the photos. We concluded that she had felt embraced, that she had good experiences from the care she had received, however abrupt the changes had been.

In our effort to understand Maria we remembered the concept that John Bowlby had described in the post-war years, abandonment syndrome, and its three stages as described above. Maria did not display actual protest reactions, but we did witness a convincing grieving process followed by a detachment, which we observed in her many attempts to "run away".

Part of the model we use at Skodsborg is to work with "what we see" and "what we know" (Thormann & Guldberg, 1995), and in Maria's case we knew very little. We are not supposed to make guesses about children's stories but to use what we know, and we need to take our observations seriously, share them with each other and reflect on what we see. We observe, we analyse our observations, we make an intervention plan, and subsequently we evaluate the intervention. We do it again and again, as the following example illustrates.

Maria's primary caregiver Rita:

At least once a day, Maria and I went for a walk in the wood. We always took the same route. Over to the wood, then down to the lake and the ducks. Before the walk we had been to the kitchen to pick up some duck food. Not surprisingly, her first word was "quack-quack".

When we were getting dressed I always said, "We're going to the wood to feed the ducks. The ducks go 'quack-quack'". One day Maria suddenly said "quack-quack" when I said that we were going over to the ducks.

When I look back and check with our diary these walks fall into three stages. The first month or so she would run far away when I took her out of her pushchair. She ran fast and without a goal. She ran down the footpath towards the lake or into the wood. She ran without looking back and without responding when I called her name. I let her run a small distance, but then I caught her up and put her in the pushchair. Maria showed that she did not want to be caught up, and that she did not want to go back into the pushchair. She twisted and turned and yelled out angrily.

After a little over a month, there was a change, as Maria began to look back over her shoulder when she ran. She still ran fast and far, but she stopped from time to time and looked back. I felt that she was checking whether I was actually following her, whether I was still there. She began to respond when I called her, stopping and smiling at me, but as soon as I approached her she would run. She showed that she expected to be caught and laughed when I grabbed her. In stage three, after about two months, she ran less far before stopping and looking back. She invited play, wanted me to run after her and catch her. If I was too slow she would run back towards me with a big smile, and when I picked her up in my arms her body was soft and relaxed.

In our common professional understanding of what Maria showed us we also drew on Per Schultz Jørgensen's theoretical model about the balance between stress, vulnerability, consequences, and protective factors (Jørgensen, Ertmann, Egelund, & Hermann, 1993). In Maria's story, the stress factors are striking—the many losses. Per Schultz Jørgensen's model helps us understand that there were also many protective factors in her life. After she was discovered in her home country she was looked after, fed and clothed, and received care (see the model in the next chapter).

In terms of Maria's vulnerability/resilience balance, based on our observations we have to say that she has clearly developed resilience. Stresses in life can become important positive experiences if the stressful situations have also involved supportive care. In the model, this is called "protective measures". When these measures are in place, the risk of negative consequences is reduced (Thormann, 2009).

CHAPTER EIGHT

A theoretical model

The interaction between stress factors and risk

At Skodsborg we have long relied on Per Schultz Jørgensen's model about the interaction of stress factors, vulnerability, consequences, and protective factors. The model has become part of the model we use at Skodsborg. It has also been incorporated into our internal work with infant therapy, and it is in use at The Family House in Horsens.

In 1993, Per Schultz Jørgensen and colleagues carried out a research study of at-risk children. The theoretical model stems from this study.

The issues are well-known, but that does not make them any less challenging. How do vulnerable children develop resilience to be able to overcome the stressful experiences they encounter in life? There is no simple answer, as the factors interact in immensely complex ways, but by analysing concepts and issues we can uncover ways of developing preventive strategies.

Our work with the theoretical model gives rise to a new question: How can the child best activate her resources? Are we, in our care, therapy, and classrooms, ready to meet the individual child exactly at the point where she makes optimal use of her potential resources? Whether this is the case or not depends in part on the balance between challenges and potential resources. Both anxiety and security can either hinder or facilitate the process. Development is a possibility, but the process may also involve stagnation and setbacks.

The main emphasis in the study was on analysing causes and symptoms in connection with stressful childhood conditions. The analysis focuses especially on social and psychological aspects and is based on some 120 Danish and international studies, mainly performed between 1985 and 1993. The analysis clearly shows that research approaches have changed. Previously, research findings typically indicated linear cause-and-effect relations, but the trend is increasingly towards also including individual reaction patterns. This has led to a circular view of cause-and-effect, as illustrated by the simplified model below.

The model

The arrows indicate that this is to be viewed as a dynamic whole consisting of interdependent parts. For example, the current stress in a person's life can be reduced by means of protective factors, which may result in diminished vulnerability, which implies that the person has reduced resilience. "Early stress factors can lead to a sort of vulnerability that diminishes the child's ability to deal with subsequent stressful experiences—which may then cause permanent damage. An early stress factor, however, may also lead to improved resilience, which in turn improves the resources for dealing with subsequent stressors" (Jørgensen, Ertmann, Egelund, & Hermann, 1993, p. 9 [translated for this edition]). That was 1993, in a study initiated by a governmental committee on children's living conditions. What initiatives do we see in the field today?

The model in relation to continuity and discontinuity in a residential institution for children

The studies carried out at Skodsborg (Thormann, Boesen & Nielsen, 1990; Thormann & Guldberg, 2003) indicate that disruptions in the relationship between a child and the child's attachment figure(s) is a stress factor that leads to increased vulnerability and reduced resilience. This is expressed in a variety of symptoms, and the child's vulnerability

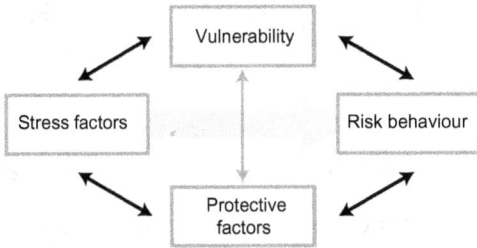

Figure 1. Model of the interaction of stress factors and risk factors (Source: Jørgensen, Ertmann, Egelund, & Hermann, 1993).

is further increased if the child experiences yet another disruption in the relationship with an attachment figure. In that case, the child will develop a more general vulnerability.

When we speak of disruptions, we use the term broadly. Disruptions may thus occur in everyday routines, for example when a substitute teacher steps in to look after a group of children while the regular staff attends a team meeting. The children will of course react to this, unless there are protective factors in place to reduce the stress: the substitute teacher is the regular substitute for this group; she is familiar to the children; she is kept up to date about developments in the individual children and in the group; when the regular staff return from the meeting the substitute teacher briefs them on how the children have been while she was with them. The overlap before and after the substitute teacher takes over is an important protective factor that makes the environment more predictable for the children. However, disruptions may also involve:

• a sudden break in a child's otherwise regular contact with the parents;
• losing one's primary caregiver;
• going to live somewhere else.

Institutionalised children often face a wide range of stressful situations, which may lead to increased vulnerability. The studies at Skodsborg have found that children who are institutionalised early in life have a much greater sense of continuity in their life than children who are institutionalised at the age of three to five years or later. Early intervention ensures general care for the child and thus reduces the stress factors and in turn promotes resilience.

The balance between protection and stress

At a residential institution, incorporating this theoretical model helps simplify many concerns and makes it easier to decide on concrete actions. The balance between stress and protection is a natural and integral part of everyday work at Skodsborg. We attempt to balance the scale by achieving a healthy ratio of protection to stress. Incorporating this model as a shared tool in the team helps simplify our collegial communication.

Case: Marcie

Marcie, who is five years old, has fallen in the playground and hurt herself. She is bleeding from a small cut in her forehead. She is startled when she sees the blood on her hands. The staff decide to take her to the emergency room to have the cut seen to. This is clearly a stressful situation for Marcie. How can we alleviate it? By introducing protective factors.

When the staff has incorporated the stress/protection model and the mindset it represents, certain factors are given in the specific situation, which we do not need to debate because we all share the same frame of reference.

Marcie is generally a vulnerable child, born with neonatal abstinence syndrome and referred to a residential institution straight from the maternity ward. She is particularly vulnerable in the specific situation, because she experienced a car crash at the age of four years, with a great deal of blood and without support, because the adults involved were unable to assist her.

Protective factors include telling her what has happened, and what the staff have decided to do about it. Among the present staff members, the one that Marcie is closest to is selected to accompany her. We order a taxi so that Marcie can sit in the backseat together with the teacher. We make sure that she takes a transitional object, in this case the mother's scarf. We contact the mother and finally the emergency room to prepare them for handling the situation with consideration for Marcie's general and specific vulnerability. This gives the ER staff the best basis for helping Marcie with her injury in a way that accommodates her vulnerability. Marcie has a positive experience, as the protective measures help her overcome the stress of falling and hurting herself and then going to the ER. Throughout, we use the method of infant therapy in a continuous flow. Here, the verbalisation becomes an essential protective factor.

Case: Matt

Matt's parents are visiting. We can tell that the mother is under the influence of drugs. We know that three-year-old Matt can also tell. However, Matt is excited to see both his parents. It has been a long time since the parents were last here to visit. Should we ask them to leave?

We relate the situation to the stress/protection model. We reach a decision. Throughout the parents' visit, a staff member is on the side line, which enhances the protection and reduces the stress. Since we know that Matt registers his mother's state, the primary caregiver uses the method of infant therapy in her words to the child: Because of the way that mummy is today, I am going to be present the whole time, until we say goodbye to mummy and daddy.

Maria's case related to the theoretical model

In the case story about Maria (pp. 74–80) the stress factors she faces are very obvious. She loses her caregivers repeatedly. First her birth mother/parents, then the caregivers in one orphanage and then another, and then her adoptive parents. However, there are also many protective factors in place for her. From what we know, she has had a gentle transition from the second orphanage to her adoptive parents. The people around Maria have looked after her personal belongings, which serve as transitional objects to her, and this is also the case when she is transferred to Skodsborg.

At Skodsborg she receives educational and psychological treatment, and she receives infant therapy, which gives her a high degree of protection. Maria gradually gets to know her new family, and her primary caregiver at Skodsborg, Rita, has remained in her life as a close friend of the family. In addition, Maria and her new family have visited Skodsborg several times. This has helped Maria to develop a sense of continuity in her life despite the changing caregivers. Maria's mother, father, and big sister have done everything they could to help Maria gradually become a fully integrated member of the family and to help her thrive on all developmental dimensions. Maria has remained a vulnerable child, but her vulnerability is increasingly giving way to resilience, and this reduces the risk of negative consequences in the form of risk behaviour.

Maria, Marcie, and Matt all presented the interdisciplinary team at Skodsborg with major challenges. However, the Skodsborg model always suggests ideas for what is the most helpful approach for the child. This theoretical model is an essential component of the Skodsborg model, and when we sit down with a pencil and paper we can quickly outline a given situation and determine what is the best approach.

Another component of the Skodsborg model draws on inspiration from Donald Winnicott's theories about transitional objects and transitional phenomena.

CHAPTER NINE

Transitional objects and phenomena and their role as protective measures

Donald Winnicott

The theory of transitional objects and transitional phenomena was formulated in the early 1950s by the English paediatrician and psychoanalyst Donald W. Winnicott (1896–1971). The theory springs from Winnicott's fascination with the interaction between the inner and outer worlds and the nature of illusions.

Winnicott's theories are informed by his own studies of infants and slightly older children. Contemporary theorists were reserved in their reception. With a touch of condescension he has been described as someone who held a deep fascination with Winnie the Pooh. He replied that his focus is of course not on Winnie the Pooh or on Linus' security blanket, and that it is not the chosen object that holds his interest but rather the purpose it serves. Winnicott noted that the first special item that a child takes possession of holds unique importance to the child, which the parents accept. He called this the child's first "not me" possession.

Sooner or later in a child's development we observe that one or more "not me" objects are interwoven into the child's personal fabric. Some children stick their thumb in their mouth, while the other fingers caress a particular part of the face. The other hand may grasp an external object, for example the corner of a sheet, a pillow or a blanket, rubbing it, often in the nose or mouth region, but there are countless other combinations. Winnicott imagined that thoughts or fantasies are associated with these experiences and referred to all these things as transitional phenomena.

If we look at the individual child we find that out of all this, there is one thing or phenomenon that appears which is crucial for the child to use before falling asleep and as a defence against anxiety. This could be a pillow, a dummy, a blanket, a song or a phrase, and these are transitional objects or phenomena. Typically, this object maintains its importance, and parents and other caregivers are aware of its value and bring it when the child has to leave his safe environment, for example to see the doctor, spend a night away from home, go on a trip etc. The transitional object thus helps give the child a sense of continuity, and this lets us use the transitional object to prevent experiences of disruption. In this sense, the transitional object becomes a protective factor. The transitional object is often respected to a degree where it is allowed to become dirty, even smelly, because it is obvious that if, for example, a security blanket is laundered it will lose its value, which the child will perceive as a disruption; a disruption that robs the object of all or some of its value in the eyes of the child. The child clearly shows how important the transitional object is, and in a healthy development the object gradually loses its importance.

The Skodsborg model expands on Winnicott's theories in a number of ways. Among other things, we always notice if a child has one or more items that he is particularly attached to or fond of. If a child has just a single object that he displays even a minor degree of attachment to we will attempt to increase the importance of the object for the child. We do this by attributing the object value, showing tenderness towards it and making sure that it is with the child in the pram or bed. If it is a teddy bear or a doll, we may swaddle it or make clothes for it. If it is a toy, we may find a nice box to put it in. We presume to believe that inanimate objects can be animated when we attribute value to them. Adults may refer to something as having sentimental value. By this we mean that the thing is charged with emotions because it reminds us of past experiences. These experiences may involve all sorts of situations and be associated with people, places or events. As adults, most of us are able to recall positively charged memories about what things have meant to us in our everyday life or in particularly difficult situations. Even as adults we may find ourselves in the borderland between our inner and outer worlds. We can use this experience in our work with children.

The transitional object and infant therapy

At Skodsborg, the staff have always practiced speaking with the children. They have "put into words" what is happening right now, what is about to happen, that mummy is coming to visit today, or that she has failed to show up. We have always been aware that this verbal communication with the child holds special value. This meant that the staff were ready to embrace the new ideas from Dolto and Eliacheff, as these ideas were quite compatible with their existing practices. For of course the children understand what we tell them, also what we convey in words.

When we first began working with infant therapy, we soon found that the child's transitional object "took part" in the therapy and thus played a key role. In relation to infants we found that the child's transitional object offered support when we told the story about mummy. Thus, it was our experience that the two "protective measures", infant therapy and the use of transitional objects, mutually supplement and enhance each other in our work with the child.

Case: Nick

Nick was born to Susan, who was a drug addict. He was born with serious withdrawal symptoms and underwent a ten-week detox programme. Thus, Nick was in a very bad way. Susan was in prison during the last part of her pregnancy. After spending two days with her newborn child, she returned to prison. Her visits with Nick were subject to available prison staff and transportation.

Nick was referred to Skodsborg, and the teacher who had been appointed as his primary caregiver, Tina, was able to visit him in hospital and gradually get to know him.

The first few weeks, Tina did not manage to see the mother at the neonatal ward. Therefore she wrote a letter to Susan. She wrote that she was assigned to Nick as his primary caregiver, and that she would like to meet Susan to discuss important issues in relation to their cooperation about Nick's care. In the letter, Tina suggested that the next time Susan visited Nick in hospital she should take off her T-shirt and leave it in the cot with her child, because his mother's scent would help Nick. The staff at the hospital told Tina that Susan was clearly touched when she read

Tina's letter. She pulled off her T-shirt and left it with her little boy.

When Tina first met Nick she used the principles of infant therapy, and throughout the process she received close supervision from the psychologist at Skodsborg (IT). She introduced herself to him, told him that she would visit him many times, and that one day, when he did not need medication anymore, he would come to live at Skodsborg, where she would look after him.

Tina was respectful in her contact with Nick, who was hypersensitive to sensory stimulation due to his withdrawal issues. She maintained a certain physical distance, spoke softly to him and told him his story. She said that he might be wondering where his mummy was. She told him that his mother was in prison, which was the reason why she could not spend as much time with him as she would like to.

"She has a hard life, but that has nothing to do with you. Your mummy loves you. When she is released from prison she is going to visit you at Skodsborg. You are always going to hold her in your heart".

Tina picked a song that she sang to him, softly, again and again. This gave Nick a transitional phenomenon. The song was used for saying hello, for saying goodbye, and as a comfort when he had his nappy changed, which seemed unbearable to Nick because of his sensory sensitivity.

One day when Tina visited Nick she noticed the grey T-shirt lying close to Nick's head. That was mummy's T-shirt—a transitional object. Tina told Nick about the purpose of the transitional object. She talked about Nick's mother while she let him sense the grey T-shirt. She carefully pulled the fabric between his palms and around his nose/mouth region. Nick showed Tina that he enjoyed their little therapy sessions where Tina used transitional phenomena, transitional objects, and the method of infant therapy on every visit. He showed it by turning his face towards her voice and by the fact that his body calmed down.

Nick developed an attachment to his mother and to Tina. When he missed his mother he snuggled with her T-shirt. When he missed Tina the secondary caregiver put his longing into words, and Nick showed his relief.

When Nick was eleven months old, Tina had to take three weeks' summer holiday. We knew that this would be a difficult time for him. For a few weeks before they were going to say goodbye Tina wore a little cotton scarf day and night. When she said goodbye to Nick she told him that she hoped that he would be able to use the scarf while she was gone. The scarf became a fixture in his bed along with his mother's T-shirt. One day halfway through Tina's holiday Nick was sitting on the floor in the living room, looking sad and introvert. His secondary caregiver, who was feeding an infant, noticed and said to him, "Nick, I think that you're thinking of Tina". The words helped Nick. He quickly crawled into the bedroom, pulled himself up by the side of the bed, grabbed the corner of the scarf and pulled it towards him. With the scarf he then crawled back to the living room and sat down in the same place, now snuggling with Tina's scarf. The caregiver said, "I know that you miss Tina. How nice that you have her scarf". Nick was seen with his feeling, and the feeling was validated.

Early referrals as in Nick's case offer good opportunities for attachment and clearly also for frustration. In a residential institution life's challenges are always present, as the primary object of love disappears time and time again, whether it is the parents or the professional caregiver. In our view, therefore, infant therapy, transitional phenomena, and transitional objects are especially important for an infant or young child in residential care. We help the child pick an object that becomes the preferred object for some time, long or short. We have learned that it is impossible to predict what the child is going to choose.

Nick, continued

An important part of the story about Nick and his transitional objects is that to Susan, Tina's letter was testimony that Tina/Skodsborg were willing to acknowledge her role as mother and to cooperate with her about her child. As Nick's mother she was consulted, she was a partner in the process, and she was taken seriously. Susan later said that she perceived the letter as an invitation, which she accepted. Susan was fully behind the idea of transitional objects to "help children handle transitions". Whenever she visited her boy at Skodsborg, she would put on the T-shirt. When she noticed a curious look she said, "Hey, it's like a battery, you need to recharge it!" When Nick transitioned to a foster family the T-shirt played an important role. It was brought along for his first visits, and it was especially crucial when he took his first afternoon nap in the new home. The foster parents saw how dependent Nick was on his transitional object and respected it. For one and a half years the T-shirt was a fixture in Nick's bed in the foster family, and before Nick fell asleep he would hold it close to his neck, mouth and nose. One day Nick insisted that it be put in a drawer, and so it was.

In the story about Nick, the experienced teacher Tina uses the methods that characterise infant therapy. She also uses the method in specific everyday moments. She does this under the supervision of the psychologist (IT), who has put together the words for the therapy. The letter to the mother was co-written by the teacher and the psychologist, and throughout the process the two maintain a close collaboration.

Case story: Dennis

Dennis arrived at Skodsborg at the age of three and a half years, accompanied by a social worker. The previous night, his mother had hanged herself after a fight with her live-in partner. That night, Dennis was looked after by a friend of his mother's who lived in the same building, and he had spent the night there. Dennis had been told that his mother was dead. He was sad and withdrawn. He came without any luggage, only the clothes he was wearing.

We contacted the mother's partner, and through him we were allowed into the flat a few days after Dennis' arrival at Skodsborg. Dennis, his primary caregiver, Kirsten, and I (IT) went to the flat. We sat in the sofa in the living room and looked around. It was a cosy home, with much attention to detail. It was obvious that the mother had taken pride in her home, and we saw that she had been fond of potted plants. There were pictures on the wall and little doilies around the living room. We put our observations into words. Dennis listened, and both he and the mother's partner told us stories about the mother. We packed some things for Dennis to take, including photographs of Dennis with his mother, Dennis at his christening and Dennis in the nursery. We also packed some toys, clothes, and other personal belongings as well as Dennis' bicycle. We took photos of the flat for Dennis' life book.

We contacted Social Services to make sure that there would be a funeral service. Due to the circumstances there was not going to be a funeral service, but we convinced the social worker who had accompanied Dennis to Skodsborg that for Dennis' sake it would be important to have a service. The service would mark an end to his life with his mother, and in the long term it would help him achieve a sense of continuity in his life. Thanks to the social worker, a very nice service was arranged. Dennis, Kirsten, and I (IT) were there, and after the service we had coffee and juice in the mother's flat. In the days following the funeral, the mother's partner visited Skodsborg several times. We also encouraged the mother's friend to visit, but she did not want to come. Later we visited Dennis' pre-school and helped him say goodbye to his friends there. Throughout this construction effort we took lots of photos and collected various materials, including a postcard of the church, a printout of the pastor's speech etc. Today, these things are all important elements in Dennis' life book, which helps give him a sense of continuity in his life despite losing his mother at such a young age.

In our work with Dennis we verbalised what had happened. We told him what we knew, although at the time we were not familiar with infant therapy. We wrote down "the story" to make sure that Dennis could bring it with him in life but also to make sure that anyone who looked after Dennis could tell the same story: the true story about what had happened. If Dennis had been referred ten years later, we would have used the term infant therapy about what we did. At the time, we said that we told him his own story. However, the original form had the same emphasis on the words as infant therapy does. In Dennis' case, certain words took on special importance, as we shall see.

When Dennis arrived at Skodsborg he wore a home-knit Faroese-style sweater in natural colours. He insisted on wearing the sweater all the time, even at night. As the days went by, he was offered some of his own clean clothes that had been picked up from the flat. Dennis accepted a change of clothes but insisted on putting his home-knit sweater back on. His mother had knitted it for him, and we felt that he still had his mother with him when he wore the sweater or when it was at the head of his bed at night when it was too warm for him to wear. For a very long time the sweater was never washed, but one day it simply had to be done. Dennis never let the sweater out of his sight while Kirsten hand-laundered it in the sink and then carefully rolled it up in a towel.

Over time, as Dennis grew, the sleeves and the body of the sweater were extended. The sweater remained his most prized possession during his one-and-half-year stay at Skodsborg, and it was an important part of his luggage when he moved in with his foster family. At that time he had recently stopped wearing it because it was too tight in several places. The sweater was pressed, and with the sleeves folded in an embrace it was placed in a picture frame and hung over his bed. When we gave him the picture at his final therapy session I told him that I could understand why the sweater was so important to him. He looked at me questioningly, and I said, "Your mother has knitted love into every stitch".

Five years later, Dennis came to Skodsborg for a visit. He had asked to speak to his "own" psychologist when he was referred to a school psychologist. The reason for the referral was that he did not pay attention in class. One day, the teacher had asked him, "Dennis, what's on your mind?" Dennis had replied that he was thinking of his late mother who had knitted love into every stitch of a sweater which he had since outgrown. The teacher did not know Dennis' story, so she did not understand what Dennis was talking about and was therefore unable to help him. In the teacher's view, Dennis' behaviour was disruptive.

The foster parents had adopted Dennis. He was their child now, and they had decided not to involve the school in his background story. Dennis explained that he had answered the teacher's question truthfully, since he was actually thinking of his mother and how she had knitted love into every stitch. He said that he would never forget that sentence. Once he had wanted to write about it in an essay, a school assignment, but he worried that others might not understand.

This conversation with Dennis, which took place at his initiative, was supplemented by a conversation at the school, which involved two teachers, the school principal, Dennis, his parents, and myself (IT). The teacher had requested a follow-up conversation because she had been very touched and blamed herself for the incident.

In infant therapy we often see how certain words, a sentence as in Dennis' case or a gesture as in Simone's case take on special meaning over time. The therapist's ability to empathise with the child's emotional state seems to increase the chances of this occurring. In Denis's case, our respect for his transitional object, the sweater, was paramount. The respect we showed him facilitated his ability to trust us.

In our daily work, we often link Per Schultz Jørgensen's model with Winnicott's theories, and the staff at Skodsborg incorporate these theories into everything they do. Children who are institutionalised or placed in foster care are more exposed to stress factors such as loss and uncertainty than other children. For these children, the transitional object (a teddy bear, for example) and the transitional phenomenon (a favourite song or story) are indispensable.

CHAPTER TEN

Therapy with infants: how is it possible?

The description of examples from practice combined with theoretical and therapeutic reflections may be inspiring for the reader, just as Dolto's and Eliacheff's descriptions have inspired us. However, the discussion of infant therapy raises several key questions. What is it that is effective? How can we explain the child's improvement? Does it even make sense to talk about psychotherapy with an infant when the infant does not have the competences that we traditionally consider a condition for therapy? This chapter will attempt to address these questions, both by examining the infant's competences and by describing "the therapeutic space" that is created in the therapeutic situation.

The infant's competences and the therapeutic space. T. Berry Brazelton

Infants have no language and are therefore unable to speak about their life. They also do not have a capacity for abstraction and symbolic functioning, they are unable to engage in a therapeutic alliance, and they have no capacity for insight. However, children have a language of their own, which consists of a behavioural repertoire that is far clearer and can be interpreted with far greater specificity than we have previously realised. T. Berry Brazelton has been a pioneer in conveying the understanding of infants as unique and independent individuals who contribute actively to their own development and their relations to their surroundings. Brazelton developed the Neonatal Behavioral Assessment Scale, normally referred to simply as the "Brazelton Scale". The Brazelton Scale was originally developed in 1973 at Harvard University in Boston as a method for observing infants under two months of age (Brazelton & Nugent, 1995). One of the purposes of the scale was to structure clinical observations and identify how babies contribute to the development of the parent–child relationship. A key condition was the discovery that it is possible to distinguish six different states of consciousness in infants (Brazelton, 1984; Munck & Poulsen, 1984). The six states are deep sleep, light sleep, drowsy, alert, alert and active, and crying.

The principle of the Brazelton Scale is that the baby's behavioural repertoire should always be assessed in relation to the current state, and that the professional should attempt to determine what the baby is capable of under *optimal* conditions. For example, one should not test the baby's ability to shut out negative stimuli when the child is "alert and active" but rather when the child is in a state of "light sleep", a state when the child naturally needs this ability. Thus, the professional engages in an active interaction with the baby during the observation, which is one feature that makes the method stand out in comparison to other observation methods. The idea is that in her interactions with the environment, especially with the parents, the baby will normally encounter such an attempt at providing optimal conditions for communication; hence, a traditional observation approach where the professional acts as a neutral and passive observer will not provide a typical impression of the baby's behaviour, since that is very atypical adult behaviour (Brazelton & Nugent, 1995).

The scale consists of a large number of items, which serve to structure the observation. The baby's behavioural repertoire is thus assessed based on twenty-eight behavioural items, such as irritability and activity level. For each item, the baby is scored on a nine-point scale. The baby's neurological condition is assessed based on eighteen reflex items, including sucking and grip, which are scored on a four-point scale. A series of additional items are used to assess at-risk or vulnerable babies. The scale does not produce an overall score. Instead, the findings can be used to describe the baby in relation to four dimensions of functioning:

1. *Social-interactive capacity*—being attentive and reactive in relation to the environment.
2. *Motor capacity*—maintaining adequate muscle tone, controlling motor activity, and performing integrating movements.
3. *State regulation*—remaining in an appropriate state under varying stimulation, for example staying awake or remaining asleep for a sustained period.
4. *Autonomic capacity* (physiological reactions)—maintaining a certain resilience in relation to external influences.

The method is used in a variety of contexts, including diagnostic assessments and assessing whether there are special concerns to be addressed in the care for the newborn baby. The Brazelton Scale also has therapeutic uses in connection with difficulties during the first month of life. Again, the basic premise is that the newborn child is a unique and independent individual who contributes actively to the parent–child relationship by expressing immediate needs and, more indirectly, by "guiding" the parents more or less effectively in providing care. In that sense, the baby has his own language in the form of a comprehensive activity and behavioural repertoire that offers a fairly nuanced representation of the baby's life and wellbeing. Infants who for some reason express themselves more vaguely may, however, need help to be seen more clearly, and that is where professional observation becomes relevant.

The trained professional is able to clarify even very subtle signals, and by performing the observation while the parents are present she can serve as a sort of interpreter for the baby. This often succeeds in giving the parents a more nuanced understanding of their child, with regard to both resources and challenges. The effectiveness of the method also consists in the special therapeutic space that the observation format helps to create. Hanne Munck describes this aspect based on her work at the Copenhagen University Babylab, Centre for Infant Research:

> A key condition is to surround the child with respect. To assume a stance of serious attention that makes it possible to create a therapeutic space, in the sense of disciplined, focused attention in an

atmosphere of open, explorative, accepting, empathic neutrality. It is this space of respect, open listening, receptiveness and wonder—this sphere of possibilities—that is crucial in all development and also fundamental in the therapeutic process. In a sense, in therapy with older children and adults it is an indispensable condition for therapy—for infants it IS therapy. (Hagemann Hansen & Munck, 2002, p. 40) [translated for this edition]

For a while, the adult has to allow his activity to be determined by the infant's initiatives, and, as Hanne Munck points out, this gives the infant the opportunity to develop her own activities and actions and to complete them primarily on her own terms. Often, the parents or other adults interfere when the baby is exploring her surroundings, for example because they want to make sure the child has sufficient stimulation. However, if infants are not allowed to take in the environment at their own pace and in their own way the result may be frustration and problems in the parent–child interaction. When we provide this opportunity in therapy, it highlights the issue and provides a new and different experience, which may have a positive influence on future interactions.

When the Brazelton Scale is used therapeutically, we do not necessarily score all the items but focus instead on what it is relevant to observe in the given situation, without, however, abandoning the fundamental principles. This flexibility makes the method very appropriate for clinical work because it can be modified to match the needs of the individual parent–child couple and to a wide variety of challenges. Only trained paediatricians or psychologists can qualify to work with the Brazelton Scale. Hanne Munck was trained by Berry Brazelton as the first professional from Denmark who was qualified to administer the Brazelton Scale. Since then, many psychologist and paediatricians have completed the training. The competence that Brazelton attributed to the infant as an independent person and as a "guide" for the parents, with professional assistance, is fully compatible with Dolto's and Eliacheff's theories. The child shows the parents how to act. In therapeutic practice with infants and their parents it is crucial to establish a so-called therapeutic space and to surround the child with respect. We consider Hanne Munck's definition very accurate.

Everybody senses a "therapeutic space" and is affected by it, including the infant. In the therapeutic space the child is allowed to be himself without being met with the usual expectations and demands. The child is met with whatever potential he has; the child is contained. The infant senses this, understands the therapist's accommodating stance and opens up to contact. In our experience, positive change already often begins after the first therapy session. We share this experience with Selma Fraiberg, among others, who performed therapy with infants for many years. She too saw that when infants are the focus of therapy something happens that is without parallel in any other form of psychotherapy (Fraiberg, 1980). But what about the language and the words we give the child? Why are they considered so essential in therapy with infants? Françoise Gautré-Delay can help us with this question.

A study by Françoise Gautré-Delay

Child psychiatrist Françoise Gautré-Delay, who is attached to the centre for child and youth psychiatry at Bispebjerg Hospital, is interested in the role of language in interventions for infants in Denmark. She is inspired by the focus and importance that French health and education professionals attribute to verbalisation in working with newborn babies (Dolto, 1985b; Eliacheff, 1993). In France, there is and has long been widespread consensus that verbalisation helps position the child as a human subject and thus involves the child actively in her own life story. The assumption is that if important facts concerning the infant's origins, social conditions, and subjective reactions to these factors are left "unsaid" this may result in symptoms that hinder the child's development.

In 1994, Gautré-Delay conducted a study of professionals' use of language in situations where the authorities remove a nought to twelve-month-old child from the home. The assumption of the study was that,

> In situations where a child is removed from the home, and where the parents find it difficult to mark their presence and provide a direct impression of who they are, the professionals who are responsible for the child may in part convey this experience through the space and scope they provide for the parents in their spoken utterances. (Gautré-Delay, 2000, p. 72) [translated for this edition]

The pilot study was based on seven interviews with a broad range of professionals working in social affairs and health services. In a situation where an infant is removed from the home, perhaps without the parents' consent, the professionals are required to preserve a sense of continuity in the child's personal history and to help the child relate to his origins and roots. The child needs help to establish symbolic markers, for example in the form of parting rituals, even if he does not cognitively comprehend the social rituals, for example the meaning of saying "goodbye". "In this situation, the key is to find a way to position the child in a cultural space, a symbolic position, for example in relation to separation, and to assign the child a space that renders him or her a human subject" says Gautré-Delay (p. 73) [translated for this edition].

Inspired by the work of Lacan and Dolto, Gautré-Delay's main focus was on examining the way the professionals related to the child through language.

> Once the decision to remove the child is made, the professionals should be able to establish the space that will allow the child to integrate his or her personal history. For the symbolic markers to be operative once the child begins to acquire language, these markers need to be firmly anchored with the significant adults in the child's environment. This means that the professionals need to indicate that they acknowledge the child's origins in the way they address the child. Through language, they can help the child maintain a relationship with the parents and their history, despite the separation. Thus, the separation is symbolised rather than becoming fixated in an imaginary relationship with the parents, which would hamper the individuation process. The term "imaginary" should be understood in its psychoanalytic sense here, referring to the fascination with an image. This fascination leads to a fixation in ideal relationships and hinders the liberation from the power of the image. The image may be replaced by certain individuals who thus, in the imaginary relationship, gain power over the person's mind. The hypothesis is that by using the professional as a "third party", the child may, through triangulation, gain symbolic support to structure his or her subjective identity. Thus, by engaging relationally, the professionals also help the child gradually learn that some of the affects and anxiety that might overwhelm the child in connection with the removal from the home can be symbolised by means of language. (Gautré-Delay, 2000, p. 73) [translated for this edition]

Gautré-Delay's study involved a series of questions related to the professional interviewee's work with infants who were removed from the home, with our without the parents' consent. The seven interviewees were all attached to either a residential institution for infants or the hospital's paediatric ward. The study found that all the interviewees described a meeting with the child in the form of a dialogue. The word *dialogue* is used here in Lene Lier's definition:

> The mother intuitively creates a structure during these initial conversations with the child by switching between talking and smiling and waiting for the child's "reply". Thus, a dialogue develops during the child's first months of life where the child varies between listening to the mother and replying with smiles and babbling. (Lier, 1999, p. 21) [translated for this edition]

All the professionals in the study felt that the infant grasped what they said even though the child did not understand language. They all agreed that this was not by cognitive means, since the infant did not understand language. The interviewees all viewed the infant as a social individual from the outset, that is, as someone who is not merely the object of care and nurture. They had adhered to a few social conventions, but only one of the seven had introduced herself to the infant at the first meeting and explained who she was, and why she was there. None of the interviewees had spoken to the infants about their life story, where they came from, or their origins. However, they all used language to help them structure the child's everyday life and as an invitation to dialogue.

What matters is the *meaning* that the professionals convey in language, and which they feel fairly confident the infant understands, although they do not believe that the infant understands the specific words. By addressing the child with meaningful words they assign the child a position in our world of social communication and address the child as entitled to this position. In practice, this means that we introduce ourselves to the infant the first time we meet, or that we explain what we are doing when we pick up the child to change a nappy. This is actually a matter of establishing a polite interaction, even with an infant.

For example, a social worker and a teacher from one of the residential institutions for infants described how an infant who had long been unsettled calmed down completely the first time she was told that her adoptive family was coming to visit her. They both had the sense that the child had grasped the meaning of the message. They too had long been waiting for this development in the child's life. It is hard to draw these conclusions with certainty. But clearly, the professionals "understood" their own message, and perhaps they were initially relieved to hear the news, and were therefore able, with their words, to resolve a burdensome uncertainty. Thus, the child achieved a greater sense of calm and structure through the words that were spoken.

> The spoken word positions the subject in language, and the subject exists by virtue of his or her words. This means that language leaves an unconscious trail in the child by virtue of the words that the people around the child say to him or her and thus is assigned a specific position that he or she will later be able to speak from. These utterances may for example include an acknowledgement of the child's origins. (Gautré-Delay, 2000, p. 75) [translated for this edition]

The term "origins" refers to the fact that every child's life stems from a woman and a man, who each have their own history. The story of the child's origins positions the child in a family and is seen as an anchor point in establishing the child's identity. This anchoring may also be operative in the relationship between the professionals and the infant, so that the parents symbolically maintain a triangulation of the relationship. It is assumed that speaking about the child's origins and personal history can help the professionals and the child structure some of the affects that seem overwhelming in many of the dramatic situations that occur when a child is removed from the home.

In her conclusion to the study, Gautré-Delay underscores that the communication associated with *symbolic order* is the subject of very little verbalisation and operationalisation in professional work with infants. The children must be assumed to have been subjected to a trauma in their life in the form of the permanent or long-term separation from the mother, with the inherent risk of being unable to organise the flow of impulses that the trauma causes. In many cases, the interpretation of an infant's signals focus mainly on physical needs, such as whether the child is hungry or tired. Studies show that few interpretations of the child's signals or symptoms concern the child's inner mental life and/or history. Based on Gautré-Delay's study it seems relevant to question the way professionals relate to the infant's origins through language. Only three of the seven interviewees mention mummy and daddy, and then mostly in specific messages, for example to announce that the mother is coming to visit. Whether the mother is present in the words that are said seems to hinge on whether she is physically present at the institution.

In conclusion, Gautré-Delay calls for certain key cultural aspects at the residential institutions to optimise treatment for the infants who are placed here. Her recommendations are in line with the content of the Skodsborg model and include teachers always introducing themselves to a child by stating their name and their task: "My name is Beth. I'm the one who's going to look after you". The teacher will always tell the child what is going to happen that day to prepare the child for the shifts in routines and care that occur, for example, when the teacher says goodbye to the child at the end of the working day and explains who is going to take over as the primary caregiver. At Skodsborg we also speak to the children about their parents as a natural element when the parents come to visit: "Today is Thursday, and mummy and daddy are coming to visit after we have fruit". We also talk to the child about the parents who for whatever reason do not come to visit.

In 1994 I (IT) visited Caroline Eliacheff in Paris. I had been practicing infant therapy for a while, and the main purpose of my visit was to receive supervision. It was a very rewarding visit (Thormann & Guldberg, 2003), because it was so striking when Eliacheff underlined that when infants are separated from their parents, the caregivers should talk about the parents every single day. They should mention mummy and daddy, and that was also the practice at the institution in Antony where many of Eliacheff's clients were referred from.

I had read several books by Françoise Dolto, and I was familiar with the idea that *all children hold their parents in their heart*. By articulating and thus underlining that that is the case we validate the child's origins and kinship. The Skodsborg model mentions that all children have the right to their own story and the right to have this story told regularly. This "telling" is practiced differently by the primary caregiver and the psychologist. In an everyday context, the child and the teacher look at photos of mummy and daddy and any siblings and grandparents. The photo of mummy and daddy are placed in sight of the child, and when the primary caregiver and the child talk about the parents, they both look at the photo. This happens several times a week and always in preparation for a visit. The experienced teacher may move on and add that, "Mummy didn't come today, that's the way it is. Now we'll look at her photo a little".

If the child has symptoms that suggest a heightened degree of vulnerability which may be related an early trauma, the child receives infant therapy from the psychologist. See, for example, Simone's story on pp. 20–24 and Nick's story on pp. 89–92. In Nick's case, his mother was in prison. She went to the hospital, where she gave birth to Nick, but already two days later she had to go back to prison. The primary caregiver, Tina, visited Nick in hospital as often as she could, which was about four times a week. Tina was familiar with Winnicott's theory of the importance of transitional objects and phenomena for children who have been separated from their parents. She was also familiar with the wider Skodsborg model.

Tina gave Nick *a song* that she always used to initiate their time together. And she told him the *story about his mother*, who was not here but in prison. She told him that his mother had a hard life, but that this had nothing to do with him. That she loved him and held him in her heart, just as Nick held his mother in his heart. Tina said that Nick was having a hard time, and that was why he was in hospital. He received medication to get better. She also told him about Skodsborg, the place where he was going to live once he did not need medication any longer. Here he would live with other children, and she, Tina, would look after him and help him. And once mummy was no longer in prison, she would visit him there.

Tina wanted to involve Nick's mother in a collaborative effort to help Nick, so she wrote her a letter suggesting that the mother left an item of clothing with Nick the next time she visited. Then Tina would help Nick remember her. The next time Tina visited, the mother's T-shirt was in Nick's cot, and from then on, the sensing of it combined with a talk about his mother became a key component of the ritual that Nick and Tina shared. The development was very convincing. A few weeks old, Nick turned his head to Tina's voice. He showed her that he was paying attention. He calmed down physically when Tina visited, his breathing was calmer, and if he did get upset she was able to comfort him.

The psychotherapeutic treatment was convincing, and Nick made progress. Twice, the hospital staff determined that he was ready to be released. Both times they reversed their evaluation and kept him in hospital. In our experience, hospital staff, especially the nurses, tend to embrace infant therapy and its method when they have a chance to see its potential. See the case of Eric, pp. 27–29, and Adam, pp. 41–51.

*Nick's case related to Brazelton's theories of the
infant's innate competences and Gautré-Delay's study*

Nick received help from a professional caregiver who had accepted a responsibility. She wanted to do what was best for the child that she was looking after, and she succeeded. She was embedded in a professional culture, which meant that she knew what constitutes optimal care for a vulnerable infant. Her verbal messages positioned Nick as a human subject with an active role in his own life story.

His care included many rituals, including hello and goodbye, the introduction, a transitional phenomenon (the song) and a transitional object (his mother's T-shirt), and the acknowledgement of his personal history and origins. It involves a sense of calm that promotes the capacity of speech to structure the feelings that will inevitably emerge in an infant going through a separation phase. The professional is constantly considering the child's state and calmly waiting for him to settle down and be ready. She allows the child to be who he is.

When the professional considers what is the best approach, empathises with the child's situation, and combines her professional knowledge with her empathic understanding, something happens in the "therapeutic space" that affects everyone involved. The therapeutic space can be established anywhere. But those who are present will never forget. The therapist's words to the child about the current reality not only enhances the individual participants' awareness of the child's situation but also helps them find their own position and role in the child's life and helps them structure their own thoughts and feelings. No wonder, then, that some professionals refer to the therapeutic space in relation to infants as a "spiritual space".

This answers the questions we asked at the beginning of this chapter.

We cannot know exactly what it is that works in therapy with infants, but the respect for the child and her life situation, the calm approach and atmosphere and all the elements that shape the therapeutic space affect everyone who is involved. The caregiver achieves a sense of lightness and clarity, as the therapist, via the therapy, creates a structure for the pressing emotions. The words are an important part of the therapy. The caregiver's calm and clarity have a positive effect on the child. We are convinced that it is the combined impact of all these efforts from the therapist, the caravan leader, that creates the development potential that the child did not possess at the outset.

CHAPTER ELEVEN

Infant therapy as a preventive measure

In many cases, we may be uncertain whether a particular experience has affected the child so profoundly that therapy is required. More and more, we tend to think that we should give the child the benefit of any doubts we have and initiate therapy. Knowing that the method applied in infant therapy cannot do any harm to the child provided we adhere to the guidelines we have little reason to hesitate.

That was the case with Magda and her mother.

Case story: Magda and her mother

A mother contacted me (IT). She had heard about therapy with infants and subsequently also read about the approach. She felt convinced that both she and her ten-month-old child would be able to benefit.

Background

During her pregnancy the mother had felt increasingly physically unwell, and she had symptoms that did not seem related to the pregnancy. She gave birth to her daughter, Magda. There were no complications, and from day one, Magda was strong and had a good contact with her mother. When Magda was about two months old, the mother was called in to the hospital where she had given birth. They had found that the mother was HIV-positive, and that the disease was in its early active stage. That was the reason for the undiagnosed symptoms she had noticed while she was pregnant.

She was in shock and broke down when they came home. Subsequently, the mother and child were called in for a series of test and talks. Over the coming months the mother savoured her intense interactions with Magda. When Magda was asleep, the mother was overcome by a profound sense of grief and pain. She had recently separated from Magda's father, and whenever the girl spent a weekend with her father, the mother collapsed. She rejected her natural network and insisted on being alone. She was unable to hold on to the hope that the doctor had held out to her: She was in treatment, there was hope, Magda was healthy, and so was the father. In a consultation at the hospital the doctor found the early stages of depression. The mother refused medical treatment for depression as well as offers to join social networks with others with the same diagnosis.

At the age of six months, Magda was a thriving and healthy baby, who invited her mother to engage in contact, insisting on it. When her invitations went unanswered she reached strongly. One day, Magda was on the changing table having her nappy changed. She appealed to her mother for contact, more and more intensely, but the mother did not "hear" her. Magda kept insisting on contact, screaming and kicking. Suddenly the mother grabbed a pillow and pushed it down on Magda's face.

She pushed the pillow down, but Magda kept kicking and struggling. Suddenly the mother came to and understood what she was doing. She was frightened and upset, held Magda in her arms, embracing her and apologising, saying that this was not what she wanted. It just happened. The mother–child relationship continued as before, with very strong emotional bonds. A few weeks later, the incident repeated itself. In exactly the same way, Magda pushed her mother over the edge. Again, the mother was shocked, and she realised that she needed help.

Magda went to live with her father, and the mother was hospitalised in a psychiatric ward. Before she was released from hospital she had joined a network and had several consultations with a psychologist. This psychologist mentioned infant therapy as a possibility. The reason why the mother contacted me (IT) was her sense that her contact with Magda was less intense than before. Something was disturbing the contact. This was the mother's feeling, and she said that it might be because of her feelings of guilt. What if Magda had died! After a few conversations with the mother I drew up a therapy proposal, which the mother approved. I was going to tell Magda everything that had happened. The mother came to my consultation with Magda on her arm. Magda was seated in a high chair with a brace in front. The high chair was at the end of the table, and the mother and I sat on either side of the table.

First therapy session

"Hello, Magda. My name is Inger Thormann. I am a psychologist. My job is to speak with children. Your mummy has asked me to speak with you. I know your story.

Magda, you are a wished-for child. Both mummy and daddy were very happy when they found out that you were in your mother's belly. You lay under your mother's heart for nine months. When you were born, your mummy and daddy saw that you were a strong and healthy girl. Even when you were just a few days old you looked intensely at mummy and daddy. You showed them that you insisted on being in contact with them. And you did establish good contact with both mummy and daddy. When you were two months old, mummy found out that she was sick. She was frightened and worried that she was going to die. She loved you. She so wanted to share her life with you. Mummy tried to forget that she was sick. I think that you could probably tell that mummy was upset. I also think that you could probably tell that mummy sometimes thought about her disease and the future when the two of you were together.

Magda, you made it. Even when things were difficult. You are a strong girl, Magda. That's what I wanted to tell you today".

Second therapy session

"Hello, Magda. We know each other. My name is Inger Thormann. I am a psychologist. My job is to speak with children. Your mummy has asked me to speak with you. I know your story.

Last time I told you that when you were very young your mother found out that she was sick. She was scared and sad. She thought about the future and about her disease. Sometimes it was hard for you to make contact with her. One day when she was changing your nappy you could not make contact with her. She could not 'hear' you. You called her. You yelled at her and kicked your legs.

Your mummy took a pillow and pushed it over your face. She wanted you to be calm. You kept yelling and screaming and kicking. Finally she could hear you, and she understood what she had done. Your mummy was very sorry about what she had done. She held you, hugged you for a long time and apologised. I think that you were scared when your mummy put the pillow over your head. Maybe you felt that your mummy was unable to take care of you. I think that you felt that it was difficult to breathe. Maybe you thought that you were going to die. You must have been very scared.

Magda, you are a strong girl with a strong will to live. You made it".

Third therapy

"Hello, Magda. We know each other. My name is Inger Thormann. I am a psychologist. My job is to speak with children.

I told you about the time when mummy found out that she was sick. She was upset. You could tell that something was wrong. Sometimes you could not make contact with her. One day you really wanted to make contact with her. You used all your strength. You yelled and screamed. Your mummy was sick. She could not handle the noise. She put a pillow over your face. But you kept going. You are a strong girl, Magda. You made mummy understand what she was doing. She held you in her arms and hugged you. A few weeks later it happened again. I think that once again you were very scared. Perhaps it was hard for you to breathe.

Perhaps you thought that you were going to die. You went to live with daddy. Mummy went to hospital. Mummy had a depression. Mummy was unhappy all the time. She did not know how to be happy. Now your mummy is able to be happy again. The doctor has helped her. The two of you live together again, and your contact is good.

You are a strong girl, Magda. You could tell that something was wrong. You made demands of your mummy, and what you did made her understand that she needed help. She found help. You did it, Magda".

Therapeutic reflections

Magda was a healthy little girl. Her contact was strong, in fact, she was generally strong.

She had a dramatic experience, but afterwards she did not show signs that she had suffered any permanent damage. She slept and ate as she had before, she babbled and smiled at her mother. The experience had been traumatic, but the symptoms did not emerge. When Magda was ten months old her mother asked for help to tell her the difficult story. Magda looked at me with a serious gaze, zoomed in on me and remained in contact through all three sessions—with one exception. When I said "Your mummy took a pillow ..." she looked at her mother all three times but then quickly returned to her contact with me.

The three sessions took place over a two-week period. The mother told me that after the sessions, Magda looked at her repeatedly. In these situations the mother referred to the therapy sessions, to what I had said. She said that it had been difficult, but that now everything was as it should be. "I love you, Magda. I'm not sick anymore". Almost daily for a couple of months, the two had these little exchanges, which always ended with a smile followed by a hug. The intense contact that had existed between Magda and her mother was re-established. The mother's HIV infection was kept in check with medication, she returned to work, and Magda lived with her little family, which had been reunited.

The mother asked for help for two reasons. She asked for help for her own sake because she felt guilty. She was ashamed about what she had done to her child. But she also asked for help for her child's sake. She was worried about a potential delayed reaction from Magda. "How much later", she asked in our initial conversations, "might Magda react?" The answer is that we cannot know. We cannot know whether she will react or how she might respond. We also cannot know what Magda's experience of the situation was. The closest we can get is the mother's perception of what she thinks Magda's experience was, combined with the mother's description of what actually happened. A report from the family's visiting nurse confirms the mother's story, as does the doctor who examined Magda after the second incident. "Everything that is left unsaid ties up energy", says Caroline Eliacheff. In the infant therapy process Magda hears her story. She is remarkably focused, considering her young age. After most therapy sessions we find that the child improves. We cannot say the same in Magda's case, as she was not displaying any symptoms of the dramatic incident. However, the contact between mother and child grew strong again. Remarkably strong.

PART II

CHAPTER TWELVE

Using the method of infant therapy with older children

The theoretical background for therapy with older children

As we worked with Françoise Dolto's approach to infants we became aware of her description of therapy with older children who have had traumatic experiences before they acquired language. Based on the method we use in therapy with infants we developed an approach aimed at older children. In this therapy format, the parents are present as witnesses while we tell the children their life story and then support them in symbolic expression, for example through play, by drawing, playing with clay or in Sandplay (see p. X). This lets the children express their inner imagery as they activate their full sensory repertoire: visual imagery as well as their sense of hearing, taste, smell, and touch. Symbols can be expressed in other formats besides words. That is, after all, what infants do. According to Dolto, children should not undergo lengthy therapy processes, which may be appropriate for adults. When working with children, we should strive to identify the right means and words as quickly as possible in order to ease the child's pain and restore a dynamic development process. Children need help to get back on track, so that their own inherent healthy capacities can drive their ongoing development.

The therapy does not demand anything from the child. It is the therapist who has something to tell the child, after thorough preparations in cooperation with the parents. The child feels seen, heard, and met. We see entrenched patterns loosen up, and the child regain his trust in life. Child therapy is aimed at children who do not appear to be thriving around the age of three to fourteen years, and who have experienced a trauma during their first years of life. Françoise Dolto has no doubt that the child can handle the truth. It is the therapist's responsibility to make the parents understand that the child is fit to hear the truth about his own life. Often, it is the parents who cannot handle having the child hear the truth. Intuitively, the child already knows. Dolto is very clear on this question: "Do not let the child have therapy if there are things about his or her own life that the child cannot be told. A child can die if no one has told the child about his or her origins—the primeval scene" (Dolto, 1988, p. 20) [translated for this edition]. The child should know who conceived her in order to be able to be proud of being alive. It is not devaluing to have parents who were capable of nothing more than putting the child into the world and then had to abandon the child for one reason or another. Loving foster parents and adoptive parents are highly important for verbal communication, but our birth parents are life-giving and vitally important in another sense. The life force of primary narcissism is in the genes. The term "bad mother" does not exist in our vocabulary.

Françoise Dolto was very interested in therapy with older children, and her approach to this group is quite in line with the general direction of her work. The core of her attitude was summed up in her admonition, "Never allow the child's pain to be forgotten".

The therapist's role

The therapist should not take over the parents' role by offering instructions or care. The therapist should also not attempt to fix things or act as a guardian. That is the parents' role. The therapist is there to promote the transfer of past urges. The therapist's role is to bring out the hidden material that is causing the current problems. Further, it is the therapist's role to help realise the things that have not happened in the child's development so far, finding the means and words to ease the child's pain. Every effort is aimed at sorting out whatever risks are blocking, draining or distorting the child's development. As psychologist and psychotherapists we often have to be the ones who tell the child the truth about the primeval scene. This information will give the child renewed vitality and the strength to communicate based on his own identity.

Dolto performed her therapy sessions in her combined office and therapy room at the Parisian Trousseau hospital, which formed the setting for her therapy with children. During therapy, the child would sit at a children's table placed at a right angle to her desk. The child was free to speak if she wanted but might also display her pain in other ways, by drawing or playing with clay.

"The therapist should support the child in communicating his or her message by other means than by words", says Dolto (1988, p. 22) [translated for this edition]. If a child talks about his evil parents, it is important to know what the child means by "evil". In order to understand the child's meaning, the therapist may ask the child to draw people who are good and some who are bad. It is important that we give the child an opportunity to symbolise and that we offer the child easily comprehensible symbols. For example, one child drew a vase with a tulip in it. The tulip drooped limply down the side of the vase. The child explained, "My mother is almost always tired".

As therapists we need to observe, see, and sense what the child's behaviour tells us. Perhaps the child knocks over the paper basket. The therapist might say, "You're showing me that you like to come here. You knock something over. It's the paper basket; it was full of stuff, which is now all over the floor. I think that you're trying to tell me something with what you just did. You're the one who knows what it is you want to tell me. I have seen your action and I know that you did it to tell me something". What is repressed will continue to come back to the child in a different form. If the repressed material is not socially accepted, the child needs to express it with the aid of the therapist.

Dolto introduced the concept of a symbolic fee. The child had to pay for the therapy. Dolto wanted the child to come of his own volition and motivation, not because of pressure from the parents or others. The fee might be in the form of a stamp or a pebble. The stamp or the pebble meant that the child was motivated for the sessions. The child came in with the goal of working through something. Once the child had made the payment, he was free to speak. And the therapist is free to listen. In our therapy with older children, we ask the child to pay a pebble. We see that it makes a difference for the children that they need to pay for the consultation with the therapist. They often take it very seriously.

We need to see the child in her longing to be seen and put what we see into words. If we fail to see this longing, the child will continue to show us the pain associated with the difficult experiences. It takes attentive presence and professional skill to read the child's body language. The child is stuck in an unresolved feeling, unable to let go of the inner conflict before she is seen and respected by the therapist. In many cases, the child has deep, repressed yearnings.

If the child resembles someone that the parent does not like it is important to put this into words to the child, for example, "You look like your Aunt Anna, whom your mother can't stand the sight of, so you have to learn to move beyond that handicap. You have the same eyes and the same face as her". Once it is verbalised it becomes real. Children like that and then learn to live with it. If it remains unsaid the child does not feel like herself. The therapist has to help the child become herself by coming to terms with her contradictory impulses. This lets the child build a coherent inner core that enables the child to speak in her own name, from the platform of her own identity.

Traumas are ingrained in the body, and the body remembers traumas from the first years of life. Based on studies of children's memory functions, Daniel Stern (1985) formulated a theory about how an infant remembers in complete episodes/images. Each episode includes the experience of one's own activity, sensory impressions, and emotions. This is tied together to form a memory unit. Infants remember in wholes. One of the components from this memory unit may later bring the entire image to life and create an expectation of what might happen.

Example

A three-month-old child had suffered severe abuse from his father and then did not see his father for a period of five years. Child Protective Services then decided that father should be allowed to resume his visitation rights. The child gladly went to see his father together with a supportive adult. When he suddenly faced his father, the child's world fell apart. The body remembered, even though the boy had not seen his father for five years.

Caroline Eliacheff (1994) describes how early traumas produce a rift in the symbolisation process. When the specific trauma is put into words, a symbolisation can begin. As long as the cleavage persists, the child is stuck in the trauma. Her message that everything that is left unsaid disrupts the symbolisation process reminds us that as therapists we must never overlook the impact of the traumas that some infants and young children experience.

There is a risk of psychological damage becoming permanent. The child's development may be severely impaired, and the limitations may become a life-long disability for the child. We relieve the child by putting the trauma into words. The most frequent symptoms that we see in older children include concentration problems, increased vulnerability, defeatism, irritability, emotional instability, and a reduced or impaired ability to handle conflicts. The child is mentally unsettled and tense and lacks social skills.

The infant's situation is less entrenched. A younger child has a capacity to repair the damage, and if the factors that hamper a healthy development are removed, the child's own capacity can drive the healing process. In older children the situation is more difficult, because it involves years of impaired development. For these children, life can be very challenging, and if the child does not receive help there is a risk of life-long dysfunction.

Description of Peter's treatment with child therapy
and Sandplay

Peter is five and a half years old. He is physically aggressive and attacks his mother. The mother seeks help. Peter has not had any contact with his father for a few years due to disagreements. For the same reason, the father cannot be involved in the therapy process, although, ordinarily, we would involve both parents. The preschool recommends delaying his school start because Peter is unable to understand and follow instructions or messages delivered to the group. Peter isolates himself from the other children, he is constantly vigilant and finds that he is bullied by the other children. Peter cannot relate a message or an incident in a coherent manner, and the staff characterises him as sad and defeatist.

Together with Peter's mother we reviewed the traumas that Peter had experienced during his first three years of life. We reflected on how Peter might have experienced the incidents at the time. This gives the mother insight into his traumas and enables her to empathise with his experience. At the second meeting with the mother we present the therapy session plan to her in writing. Once the mother approves the message that the therapist has written down, based on the mother's description of specific incidents, the mother typically has a sense that "that is what it was like", and when we find that the mother is able to contain the child and his or her pain, the therapy can begin, with the mother present as a witness. That is also the case with Peter's mother.

The room is readied, as are the sandboxes. One sandbox contains wet sand, the other dry sand. On shelves along the wall there are figures/symbols: humans, trolls, monsters, animals, rocks, trees, houses, cars, etc. Two chairs are placed close together. One for Peter and one for his mother. At the far corner of the therapy room, a table is set; there is a wicker tray with flowers and a candle, juice, fruit, biscuits, and coffee. The therapy session opens with the introduction: "Hello, Peter. My name is Inger Poulsen. My job is to speak with children. Your mummy has asked me to speak with you". All sessions begin with these words, which signal that "I have something to tell you". In the therapy, the therapist addresses Peter directly and respectfully and puts his earlier traumas into words. Peter listens attentively. After the therapist has spoken directly to Peter, with the mother as a witness, the mother is asked to sit down at the coffee table, while the therapist and Peter move to the sandboxes.

First therapy session

"Hello, Peter. My name is Inger Poulsen. My job is to speak with children. Your mummy has asked me to speak with you.

I am going to tell you what happened when you were very young. I think that in your mind you have forgotten what happened, but 'the body remembers'. Daddy and mummy gave you life, you were created in your mother's womb. You lay under your mother's heart for nine months. The delivery went well, and you were placed at your mother's breast. You also have a big sister, who is two years older than you, her name is Hannah. Hannah looked forward to having you as her little brother. All four of you lived together at Number eight Mill Street. You also have a granddad. There are many people in your family who enjoy being with you".

Peter is invited to use the sandboxes and the symbolic figures on the shelves. He begins by making a huge pile of sand in the wet sandbox. It looks like a pregnant belly. He toils to dig out the bump, which keeps collapsing. Peter is deeply focused, he drools slightly and sighs, breathing deeply. When the tunnel underneath the bump finally stays up, Peter places a tiny Moomin troll figure inside the cave. With satisfaction, he notes that the construction is stable. He draws a deep sigh. Then he finds a mother figure and a father figure and places them in the corner of the sandbox. Next, he finds a little blanket which he carefully and tenderly folds around the little Moomin figure.

During this wordless process, Peter looks up at me repeatedly to see if I am paying attention to his process. His eyes seek mine. His relief and satisfaction are visible when he looks down again and continues his work. Peter looks at me and says, "Now this box is finished", and then moves on the to the dry sandbox. Peter eagerly and with quick movements picks a little man from the shelf. He does not look at me, but he senses that I am with him, and that I am not interfering with his work.

In my interpretation, Peter uses the small male figure that he selects from among the figures on the shelf to symbolise himself. I use this interpretation to understand what Peter is trying to tell me. I do not share my interpretation with Peter. The goal is not for the child to understand the process but to live it. The therapist's task is to remain attentive and receptive and to act as the child's witness in a respectful and appreciative manner. If I say anything at all it is to mirror what he does. When he sighs, for example, I might mirror him by sighing too. Typically, the child subsequently explains what it was all about. The scenario in the box is his. I am his witness, and I have faith in his ability to find a solution.

In the sandbox now, the evil characters have the upper hand. A small male figure is shooting a rifle. His head is loose, attached to the body with a magnet. The head falls off each time he fires the rifle and has to be painstakingly put back on. In a quiet, monotonous way he fights a brave battle. He shoots the evil characters who encircle him, but they keep getting up, even after they have been shot and buried in the sand. Peter sighs deeply as he struggles on. I observe his helpless body and follow his tireless struggle. Peter repeatedly seeks my eyes as if to reassure himself that I am with him, witnessing his struggle. My eyes assure him that I am watching, but I do not say anything, to avoid disrupting his thought process. Peter's body relaxes when he engages in his focused effort. Several times during the process he has to use the toilet. When Peter arrives for his second therapy session he arrives alert and ready to get to work in the sandboxes right away.

At the first therapy session I had informed him that one has to pay to go to therapy. My job is to speak with children. Each time I need to be paid a pebble for my work if he wants to speak with me. If he does not bring a pebble because he does not want to speak with me, I will instead tell his mother what I have to say.

Second therapy session

"Hello, Peter. My name is Inger Poulsen. My job is to speak with children. Your mummy has asked me to speak with you.

I think that you have often overheard your mummy and daddy arguing. I think that it has hurt you, because you love them both and may want them to be friends. Perhaps you are hoping that you could all live together, the four of you. Your mummy and daddy have decided to live apart. Your daddy lives with Hannah. You live with your mummy. Your mummy and daddy can tell that you are having a hard time, Peter. They want to do whatever they can to help you".

Peter looks mournfully to the sandboxes and is ready to get to work. During the first three therapy sessions, the same struggle unfolds as the one that was staged in the dry sandbox during the first therapy session, over and over again. I observe Peter's struggle. I am his witness, and I acknowledge his persistence.

Third therapy session

"Hello, Peter. My name is Inger Poulsen. My job is to speak with children. Your mummy has asked me to speak with you. I know your story.

Your mummy and daddy argued. I think it must have been hard for you. Perhaps you were scared. Your mummy went to hospital, and the police came for your daddy. I think you must have been scared. You haven't seen your daddy in a long time. Perhaps you miss your daddy. Your granddad was with you. Your mother recovered quickly and came home to you. I think you must have missed your mummy when she suddenly wasn't there.

Perhaps you were worried that she wouldn't get well again. Perhaps you were also angry with your daddy. Your daddy loved you and your mummy, but when he drank alcohol he became angry and mad. Your mummy knows that you miss your daddy. She knows that this is hard for you, and she doesn't know when you can see your daddy again. You can always hold your daddy in your heart".

After the third therapy session, a sudden change occurs. The evil figures stay under the sand when they are shot. One by one they are transformed into good figures. One figure remains evil, but the good figures had no trouble overpowering him. Peter looks at me and talks, with joy in his voice and a light in his eye about an inner reconciliation with his father, who has disappeared from his life. In a concrete enactment in the sandbox, Peter shows me how his father goes up in a helicopter and flies over to the place where Peter lived with his mother and father when he was little, a home they had to leave in a hurry. Peter tells me eagerly that daddy is in the basement, where he picks up some toys that Peter needs, and then he is going to fly back and give them to Peter.

I say to Peter that I think he loves his daddy. Peter talks about nice things that the two used to do together. After this session, Peter's Sandplay changes. He is no longer playing the same game. The good figures stay good, and Peter begins to create landscapes. The landscapes are filled with life, colours, light, joy, and people. Peter has pulled himself together and regained his footing in life. Peter had nine one-and-a-hour therapy sessions. Each time I told him a section of his story, and then he worked in the sandboxes.

The mother's impressions of Peter after the therapy sessions

Peter's mother says that his aggressive attacks on her have ceased. Peter is more open and tells her about the things that are on his mind. They share many positive moments. In preschool he has made friends, who visit him at home. The mother says that he is a different child now, a child who is full of spirit and who has faith in his own ability to succeed. In preschool, they no longer perceive him as vulnerable and now recommend that he could start school along with his peers. Peter takes part in group activities. He has a best friend in preschool and is able to focus on a task. Peter likes to play with the other children, and everyone agrees that he has made excellent progress.

All child therapy at The Family House is recorded on video. This is done both to ensure that the therapist can receive help in reading the child's signals and that the therapist can receive supervision based on the actual therapy session afterwards. At the conclusion of the therapy process, Peter and his mother review some segments of the therapy together, and after seeing some clips from the first therapy session Peter comments, "That's from the time when I was sad".

Therapeutic reflections

Early traumas had frozen Peter's body, preventing his world from becoming whole. He did not understand what was happening around him, and he did not have the capacity to engage constructively in relations. A cleavage in the symbolisation process created an entrenched situation. The father had moved out suddenly and under dramatic circumstances, which had caused Peter to be stuck and left him with a trauma. In Sandplay he symbolically acted out his struggle and his powerlessness. Eventually, the good guys won. With joy and triumph in his voice, Peter demonstrated how his father had flown back to their old home in a helicopter to collect the things that Peter was missing from the basement. Through symbolisation in play, Peter found a way to reconcile with his father and the events that had happened.

Peter was given his story. The concrete and traumatic events from the first two years of his life were told to him in a respectful and acknowledging manner: "Your mummy has told me that when your mummy and daddy argued you were all quiet and shut it all out. I think that was hard for you. I think that you loved both your mummy and your daddy. It was a good thing that you protected yourself. Now, your mummy and daddy have found a way to live their lives separately. They both want you to have a good life. Your mummy wishes that she had been better at looking after you".

Throughout the therapy process, Peter would often glance quickly at his mother, who always nodded back at him approvingly. The therapist conveyed the hope and thus contained both Peter and his parents.

To Peter, the world regained its coherence, and the symbolisation process had begun.

Sandplay therapy

Sandplay is a form of analytic symbolic therapy. It is based on Jungian psychoanalytical thinking and can be used with both children and adults. At The Family House, our main method is conversation. Language is essential. Many of the children and adults who come to see us have no experience putting their emotions into words, but we know that communication includes much more than the spoken word. Sandplay therapy enables children and adults to establish contact with events that have not become conscious, so-called preconscious material, in a symbolic narrative. Emotions and conflicts can be expressed and thus made conscious, and subsequently it is possible to develop a sense of order in the previous chaos.

At The Family House we have two sandboxes. They are rectangular, 60 cm by 105 cm surrounded by a 20 cm wall. The interior bottom of the boxes is ocean blue. They are placed in a rack with wheels. In the therapy room, a set of shelves takes up the entire back wall. This is where the symbolic figures are found. There are elements from the earth, the sky, various religions, flora, fauna, death, love, evil as well as children, adults, tables, chairs, cots, breasts, sticks, beads, food, coffins, and bridges—there are no restrictions to a Sandplay collection, but it has to contain multiple doors to the past and the future. From this diverse collection of symbols, the clients choose what to place in the sandbox. The symbols and their positioning tell a story and illustrate what is on the client's mind, and where the person's difficulties lie.

The therapist's role is to be the client's witness to the important creative work that takes place in Sandplay therapy. When a child or an adult makes an image the therapist offers his supportive presence and shows interest in the process. Mostly, the process is without words. The therapist's main task is to observe, to be present and attentive, and to notice his own impulses during the process, which may help the client in the next stages of the process. The client may choose to speak about the process and engage in a dialogue about the imagery; sometimes, however, the client may not want to speak about the imagery and the symbols.

It is very important that the symbols are placed in the sand. Already when the client chooses a symbol and decides where to place it, the client has begun to address her problem/state/pain. A healing, liberating symbolisation is taking place. Words can set us free, that is well-known. But words cannot describe very deep and early conflicts. Symbols, figures, and images can.

Sandplay is a specific nonverbal therapeutic method, where, children and adults can express their inner complexity. For example, anxiety, aggression, guilt and shame, and other painful feelings can be released through Sandplay and the selection of figures symbolising the inner conflict that led them to seek treatment. Sandplay is a relatively new therapeutic method in Denmark, and at The Family House we often combine it with infant therapy targeted at older children.

Description of Marie's storytelling therapy

Marie came to Skodsborg from the institution where she had been placed on an emergency referral after both her parents suddenly disappeared. They went to ground when the father had failed to show up to serve a prison sentence and were now wanted by the police. The grandmother contacted Child Protective Services. Marie was placed into care at the age of nine months. She soon showed convincing progress, both emotionally and cognitively. Both parents had a severely reduced parenting capacity and were involved in crime. Thus, there was no doubt that Marie would be placed in foster care.

When she was just shy of two years, Marie was placed in a foster family. She came in for two follow-up visits to Skodsborg together with her foster mother, and her primary caregiver at Skodsborg, Julie, visited the foster family twice. Ten years later, when Marie was twelve years old, I (IT) was contacted by Social Services in the town where she lived. Marie was having difficulties. She struggled with her identity. She found it difficult to live in between two families and had chosen her foster family. She wanted to be the foster parents' daughter, and she wished that she could have been in her foster mother's womb before she was born. She wanted the same last name as them and rejected her original family name.

Marie was tired of the many questions from her school mates about why she lived with a foster family, why this, why that. She was very unhappy that she had once lived in an institution. She thought that others probably perceived it as the worst thing that could possibly happen to anyone. Marie was very happy about the life she was living in her foster family, in her school, and after school. She had recently returned from a trip abroad with the foster family when I met with her and her foster mother at Skodsborg. She told me that she was one of the best students in her class. She went horseback riding in her spare time, often together with her foster mother who was herself an avid horsewoman. Marie never saw her biological father, and her biological mother was currently in prison, serving a sentence for the attempted murder of Marie's father. Marie was regularly in contact with her grandmother and her siblings.

In three conversations we talked about the part of Marie's life that I was familiar with. Marie brought her life book from Skodsborg, which consisted of two large ring binders filled with photos, stories, and letters. Julie, Marie's primary caregiver from Skodsborg, had made this book, which was clearly a labour of love and care. In the photos we saw a well-groomed, pretty, and happy little girl showing off her new red shoes. We saw her at picnics and birthday parties, blowing out the candles on her cake. In other photos she was together with family members and friends. In a plastic folder at the back of the book were letters and postcards that she had received from her family and from Julie. It had been several years since Marie had last looked in the book. She had pushed her past, her history, aside. During our talks and in the meeting with the material from her life, memories came up that were retold with a smile. The life book with the many photos brought out many memories, also for me. In one photo, Marie sits with a little Fisher Price tape recorder. She is clearly listening with rapt attention. I told Marie and her foster mother the story behind the photo.

"When you were one and a half years old, Julie was going away on holiday for three weeks. You two were very close, and you missed her when she wasn't at work. Another teacher, Eva, whom you were also fond of, was going to look after you while Julie was gone. Julie and the other teachers who looked after your wanted to do the very best for you, so that you wouldn't have any doubt about whether Julie was coming back. You had a soft doll that you loved, and who was always with you. It reminded you of Julie, because it was a gift from her. It was your "transitional object". Julie had also given you a song, which was your transitional phenomenon. But Julie had a new idea because she wanted to help you. She bought a little tape recorder and made a tape for you. She recorded your song, and on the tape she said that she was on holiday, and that you would probably feel that she was gone a very long time but that Eva would look after you while she was gone.

While Julie was on holiday the little tape recorder became a sort of transitional object for you. You carried it with you around the play room or kept it on a shelf by your bed. Regularly you would put it down on your little table, sit in front of it, and push the button. While you listened to what Julie said in the tape you kept nodding, and no one had any doubt that you understood what she said. You hummed along when Julie sang your special song. When Julie returned from holiday you gave her a warm welcome. Your relationship had remained vital. You had been understood with your sense of loss. Your feelings were taken seriously. The tape recorder and the tape remained important to you. You preferred to have it with you everywhere you went, but its proper place was on the table by your bed, so you did not bring it into the garden or on walks to the wood".

Marie remembered the little tape recorder. She still had it at home and decided to bring it next time. Marie had no doubt that she had thrived at Skodsborg, but she did not like her history. She was embarrassed about it. Therefore she sometimes pretended that her foster mother was her birth mother. When she was with her biological family she felt like a stranger. Generally, she felt "wrong". In the foster family it was not always easy, because she was not their child, even though she wished that she were. Marie would have preferred to rid herself of her history.

As mentioned, Marie's mother was in prison after a failed attempt to kill Marie's father. She had written to Marie a few times. Marie brought the most recent letter, where her mother asked her forgiveness for what she had done and expressed the hope that Marie would agree to see her when she was released from prison. Marie felt that the whole thing was very difficult. She did not know what to do.

In my work with Marie I used a combination of approaches. Conversations with Marie and her foster mother, conversations with Marie on her own, and therapy based on the method of infant therapy. We used the "vulnerability model" (see Chapter Eight). Together, we filled out the model carefully, dwelling on the individual components: stress factors, vulnerability, protective measures, and consequences. Until our meeting, Marie had mostly thought about the stress factors in her life. The model added more nuance to her understanding of her own life. She spoke to me more clearly and was more open in her facial expression and posture than she had been initially. After this stage, Marie went into therapy.

First therapy session

"Hello, Marie. My name is Inger Thormann. I am a psychologist here at Skodsborg, as I was when you first came here, at nine months old. I know your story, and you and your foster mother have told me about the part of the story that I didn't know.

Your mother and father gave you life, and your mother carried you under her heart for nine months. When you were a baby you lived with your mother and father. You were a wished-for child, and both your parents loved you very much. Both your mother and your father had other children, but you were their love child. They hoped that your birth would make it possible for them to make family life their priority and put all the bad things behind them. But that is not what happened. Your mother and father were focused on many other things besides you, and they did not look after you well enough. The visiting nurse told the authorities, and they talked to your mother and father. I think that even then, you could probably tell that something wasn't right. Your grandmother visited often. She could also tell that you were not taken care of properly. One day, your mother rang your grandmother and asked her to look after your because both your mother and your father had left. You were sleeping in your cot in the flat when your grandmother let herself in and took you in. After a few days your grandmother realised that she couldn't take you in just like that. She contacted the authorities, and you were placed in an institution, where your grandmother visited you every day. After a few weeks you moved to Skodsborg. Here too, your grandmother visited you often. I think that you could tell how much your grandmother loved you, and that she would always be there for you. We'll meet again next week, and then I'll tell you the next chapter in your story".

Second therapy session

"Hello, Marie. Today we'll continue with your story. The last thing I told you was that you moved to Skodsborg where your grandmother came to see you frequently.

You lived in group with two other children. You were a serious little girl. You followed the staff with your eyes as they moved about the room. You rarely smiled. You observed. I think that had become used to people entering your life and then disappearing again. Perhaps you were worried that it would happen again.

We noticed how happy you were when your grandmother visited, and the two of you were together. Then you were smiling and babbling. I think that your grandmother has been a very important person in your life. She saw you, she saw what you needed, and she saw that your parents weren't able to be your parents. She took over the responsibility. Your mother came to Skodsborg to visit you. When she came you had not seen her for six months. You didn't recognise her, and you were upset when she picked you up. Your mother was angry that you weren't happy to see her and thought it had something to do with your grandmother. Your mother decided that your grandmother couldn't visit you for a while. Your mother disappeared from you again, and your grandmother came back into your life, and that's how it has been. Your mother has come, your mother has left again. Your grandmother has been there the whole time, and no one can tell her that she can't be there for you. She loves you very much. It's so nice that you've had your grandmother. It's so nice that you have her".

Third therapy session
"Hello, Marie. Today, we're going to continue with your story. The last thing I told you was that your grandmother has been there for you your whole life. She is still there.

At Skodsborg you were very fond of your primary caregiver, Julie, and you bonded with her. Although Julie left you every day to go home, you knew that she would return. When you went to live with your foster family, we hoped that you could stay there until you were an adult. They were going to be your family. And that is also how it worked out. The family that you were born into is still your family. Your grandmother brings together the whole family, siblings, half-siblings and cousins once a month. She has always done that, and she will continue to do that. Your grandmother helps you hold on to your family and your extended family.

Your life has turned out the way it has. You have two families, and both families have affected you in different ways. That is your story. It cannot be changed.

I think that you will learn to live with both your families. You have already handled a lot, and you are a strong girl".

Therapeutic reflections

Marie was referred to me by Social Services in her home town. The social worker and the foster care consultant felt that Marie might benefit from a few consultations with me. I took on the task and found that Marie was stuck in her perception of her own history. The foster mother found it hard to support her because she had a deep emotional bond to Marie. It was difficult to speak about Skodsborg in the foster family.

With Marie's life book as our frame of reference we reviewed Marie's life at Skodsborg together. Marie recalled memories that had previously been inaccessible to her, and in the photos she saw that she had been happy and received care, and she saw herself in a beautiful, cosy, and caring environment where personal events and holidays were celebrated. She saw herself in a bumblebee costume at a carnival, and she saw herself next to the Christmas tree at Skodsborg, together with family members and Julie. Marie had words and images associated with her early history and what had happened in her life before she went to live with her foster family. She showed some degree of relief and became more clear and direct in her contact.

Marie's current crisis had been triggered by the most recent letter from her birth mother in prison. In the letter her mother expressed a desire for contact with her daughter and asked Marie to forgive what she had done. This seemed overwhelming to Marie. Her anger over being born to these parents was expressed in part in anger towards the institution that had cared for her during part of her early childhood. In the relatively brief series of sessions, Marie was able to sort out her history with the institution, and she heard some words describing the background for her referral. Marie also learned that no one can change their history, even if it is hard work to deal with it. A strong girl can overcome many stressful experiences. In my assessment, however, Marie would need a longer therapy process than I could offer, so I handed the case over to a psychologist associated with Special Needs Services in her local municipality.

CHAPTER THIRTEEN

The method of infant therapy and other professions

M any people in different professions and with a wide range of training backgrounds are drawing inspiration from our presentations of infant therapy and the method it involves. What is it that speaks to so many of us? If we ask the audience when we give a presentation or a seminar, many say that it feels so right. That is both grand—and common sense. The method brings about a sense of sharing whatever is in the present moment. The profound meeting between therapist and child/client feels like a mutual dance between two nervous systems. That provides a physical sensation of being on the right track. Perhaps we are nearing the essence of what it is that happens in the therapeutic present moment. When the therapist's nervous system synchronises with the child's nervous system, the child is able to "let go" of the trauma that has tied up so much energy. Many complex issues dissolve when we go back to the core and listen to what it is the child is telling us. As adults, we often neglect to listen to what the child tells us. It may seem like a simple thing. Perhaps it is something we already know but have forgotten, and perhaps that is why it feels so right, like common sense, to listen intently and try to understand life from the child's point of view.

So, what can we do to learn to listen to the child? We have to temporarily put ourselves and everything else aside, be fully present and try to see the child from the child's own point of view.

We base our approach on the assumption that the child is doing everything possible to cooperate. What was it that became so difficult for the child? What is it the child is telling us with her behaviour? Perhaps there is energy tied up in something unsaid, which prevents the child from achieving a natural course of development. What is the child's reality? It will often be helpful for the child if the adult sees the child's efforts to handle the world, and if the adult verbalises what he sees the child do, in a way that makes the child feel seen, heard, and met. It is helpful for the child when the adult offers a neutral verbalisation of the child's life and world.

This way of seeing the child is inspirational to many professionals. The individual practitioner is inspired to use the method of infant therapy in here-and-now situations. In these situations we do not use the term "therapy", as therapy is only conducted by trained psychologist and psychotherapists; however, the method of infant therapy is an important didactic tool, and we are extremely pleased to see the method applied in almost all the related areas, including social services, healthcare, day care, nurseries, and schools.

In social services

Case: Ida

A trainee social worker had attended an introduction to the child therapy approach that is practiced at The Family House in the Danish town of Horsens. That very afternoon, the social worker who supervised the trainee was contacted by a mother who had been exposed to domestic violence and threats from the children's father. Now the mother felt so threatened that she had to leave the home. Together with her daughter, ten-year-old Ida, she had left the family home in a hurry, and now they were standing on a street corner, in need of immediate assistance. The other four siblings were in their respective day care facilities and in school. On her way to the street corner where the mother was waiting, the social worker, who was already familiar with the family, told the trainee that before leaving the office she had rung the father's sister and asked her to go check on the father because she worried that he might be suicidal.

When the social worker and the trainee had met up with the mother and her daughter, they found a bench in a nearby park where they could talk. The social worker asked the mother to explain what had happened. She talked about her efforts to stay in the home despite the abuse, in part because the children were very close to their father. Now, however, the father's threats had become so severe that the mother feared for her life. While the social worker told the mother about the crisis centre and her options for assistance, the trainee was becoming increasingly aware of Ida's behaviour. Based on what she had heard that morning about the importance of involving children, putting emotions into words, and letting children know what is going to happen, she focused on Ida, who was standing on her own, behind her mother. Ida seemed frozen in place, shoulders pulled up, her gaze turned down, her whole body tensed up, while the mother was crying as she described the events.

The trainee noticed Ida's body language, which told her that Ida was frozen in a defensive response, and that the situation was extremely stressful for her. The trainee had heard the mother's description of the increasingly stressful and intense situation at home, and now she empathised with Ida's experience of a home life with violence and threats between the parents, both of whom she loved dearly. The trainee squatted down and addressed Ida directly: "Ida, I think that it's really hard for you when mummy and daddy don't get along. Now we're going to take you to the crisis centre, where you can stay until your mummy decides what needs to happen in the future. Perhaps you're also thinking of your daddy". Ida looked up and met the trainee's gaze. "We have talked to your aunt Karen. She is going to go see your daddy. We are going to talk to both your parents about where your brothers and sisters are going to stay until your parents decide what is going to happen". Ida's shoulders came down. Now she looked directly at the trainee and sighed deeply, while she melted into her mother's arms and let her tears flow freely.

The trainee's attention helped Ida. The trainee assumed leadership. She addressed Ida directly and put her observations into words. She also told Ida what was going to happen. She included Ida and treated her with respect. The experience gave the trainee a sense that this awareness gave her a way of being with children who are facing a stressful situation. Her awareness had been heightened, and she knew what to do to assist in the difficult situation Ida was facing.

In healthcare

Case: Lisa

Lisa was born to term and was released from hospital with her family four hours after she was born. Three days later, the visiting nurse came to check up on the girl. She found a very pale little girl and referred the family to the family practitioner, who in turn referred Lisa to Skejby Hospital where she was found to have a severe heart defect. Lisa was hospitalised for almost five months, had multiple surgical procedures, and during this time one of her lungs collapsed.

The visiting nurse describes the situation:

"After Lisa was released from Skejby Hospital I visited the family several times. Lisa was now twenty-two months old and was thriving. She went to Skejby Hospital for regular check-ups.

During the time that I have known the family, I have read about therapy with infants. I watched a video about the method, and I find the approach inspiring. I think that it must have been a dramatic experience for Lisa to be hospitalised for so long and to have had so many procedures. It seemed important to have these experiences and the related emotions put into words.

I asked the mother whether they had talked to Lisa about her stay at the hospital, and she said no. I asked if they had some photos, and it turned out that the hospital had given them a DVD when she was released. We looked at the photos together. A skinny little Lisa, with a tube in her nose, appeared on the computer screen. She looked scared. Lisa was upset, and the mother was quite emotional when we saw the picture. I said that the hospital stay must have been a very dramatic experience. So many things had happened that had been painful. I said I could see that Lisa was scared, and that I knew that mummy and daddy had been scared too, worried about losing their little girl. It was hard to be fed through a tube, and it hurt. Lisa had blood samples taken and was stuck with needles. She was anaesthetised and had difficulty breathing. Mummy and daddy had to let the doctors and nurses do these things even though they knew it would be painful for her. They had to do it so that she could survive. Repeatedly I told Lisa that her parents loved her very much.

Lisa gradually settled down. She came over and sat between me and her mother. She calmed down completely. The mother showed her grief that Lisa had had such a tough start in life. In the last photos on the DVD, Lisa had recovered and was ready to go home to her mother and father. I encouraged the mother to watch the photos with her daughter from time to time and to verbalise the feelings that accompanied the situations in the photos.

Afterwards, I heard that Lisa had generally settled down after looking at the photos and having them explained to her in words. To me, it seemed very convincing that she calmed down because of my intervention".

The presentation of the method involved in therapy with infants had also made an impression on a municipal supervisor for registered childminders, who spontaneously mentioned that since she had heard about therapy with infants and the underlying ideas, her perception of children and her approach to working with them had changed. A change that was very helpful in her work with the local childminders. Wondering "What's the child telling me", understanding the importance of putting the child's feelings into words, and being clear and direct in telling the child what is happening and what is about to happen—these are methods that make sense. "It feels as if the children and their needs have become more visible", she said.

Childminders have a very important job. They are the adults that the children need to bond with while their parents are at work, which often covers many of the child's waking hours. In addition, they often look after children who are very young, a period when the personality development begins and hence a sensitive period. It is crucial that childminders see the child as an individual little person and listen to what the child is expressing by her way of being in the world. It is essential to prepare the child for what is going to happen, also with infants. Childminders have a big responsibility for ensuring that the individual child feels seen, heard and met, so that the child can develop a strong and healthy inner core with faith in her own worth. At The Family House we have provided training for childminders for several years.

In day care

Case: Karen

A registered childminder told us about a girl who refused to eat. In the child's home, this was a daily cause of conflict and was becoming a major issue and a source of stress. The childminder felt that this struggle was leaking into the child's life in day care. She was looking for help to see what she could do to prevent this. We discussed the situation, and together we tried to empathise with the child's experience. What was the child showing and telling us with these protests? The next day, when the child came in, the meal situation gave rise to the usual problems. The child was thrashing about in the high chair. The same occurred if the child was sitting on the childminder's lap while she ate. It was almost as if it had become a ritual.

The following day, before the meal the childminder sat down facing the child and said, "Karen, I can tell that you are very upset when it is time to eat". Karen held the childminder's gaze for a long time. "You have to eat, and I want to help you as much as I can". Karen looked at the childminder, and the childminder did not break her gaze but waited until Karen was done with the contact. Then she fetched the food and handed it out to the other children. Karen sat still, watching her. The childminder then sat down without placing the food directly in front of Karen and said again, "I'll help you". Karen sat still for a moment, then she reached for the little squares of bread and began to eat. Delighted and astonished, the childminder rang me and said that Karen had not had any problems eating since she had verbalised the situation. She informed the parents, and they too were able to break the cycle of Karen's "refusal to eat".

Here we see that Karen is stuck in a habit. By observing Karen and putting the situation into words—while Karen also hears that she wants to help her and feels that the she actually means it—the childminder helps Karen achieve something that has been very difficult for her.

In the nursery

Case: Sophie

When we give seminars about therapy with infants, the audience is mainly made up of child care professionals, and naturally the individual participants reflect on specific children in their care. That was also the case for the nursery teacher responsible for the little girl Sophie.

The teacher said that two-year-old Sophie was always upset when it was time for her afternoon nap. Sophie was frightened by loud noises and generally fearful. The teachers discussed it and decided that the following day Sophie's primary caregiver would sit down at eye-level with Sophie and tell her that she wanted to talk to her. The teacher placed two chairs on opposite sides of a small table in a quiet room. The teacher asked Sophie to sit on one of the chairs, then took the other seat and said, "Sophie! I think that you're tired. You have played outside all day with the toy pram. I have decided that you will take your nap outside in your pram underneath the big tree. Here you can relax and listen to the birds singing. Lene, Karen, and I are her while you sleep. We'll look after you. When you have had your nap you'll get up and have some fruit. You will also have time to play a little before your mother comes to take you home". Sophie slept without any problems. The following days, they followed the same pattern. The teacher said, "Sophie, let's have a little chat" and Sophie went and picked up her own chair and prepared for the conversation, which took place in the same location every day.

Here, an adult assumes leadership and addresses Sophie directly who is told what is happening and what is going to happen. The ritual with the two chairs facing each other and the brief summary of what has happened and what is going to happen helps Sophie to overcome the anxiety that had become a routine for her. This lets her establish new routines with the teacher as a "transitional object".

In school

Case: Noah

Noah's mother received several phone calls every week from Noah's reception class teacher because six-year-old Noah had trouble controlling his temper. He often got very angry and left the school in anger, so that his mother had to go look for him. Noah's mother found that her stomach knotted every time the phone rang. When she found Noah he was usually angry. He yelled at her and refused to come home with her. When the mother insisted, he threatened her, and sometimes he even attacked her physically. The situation was very stressful for the mother.

The family consisted of Noah, his eighteen-month-old baby sister, and his mother. Six months earlier, the family had moved to a new town after the parents had separated. Noah's father was in prison, and Noah missed him. Ever since Noah's birth, the mother had had difficulty understanding his needs. Their time together was often chaotic and full of power struggles. Noah wanted the contact with his mother, but both Noah and his mother had a low frustration threshold. The family was affected by the father's drug use, which had led to both physical and psychological violence.

When Ida was born there was no room for one more child in the mother's life. She gave Ida the necessary physical care, but she withdrew mentally, which meant that Ida also withdrew from contact. She shut off contact with her mother but also with the world around her. She was often sick, refused dialogue with anyone, did not want to be held, and generally appeared as a quiet, withdrawn girl who lived in her own world.

Ida had given up, and her big round blank eyes looked straight through anyone who attempted contact. The situation at home was untenable. The mother realised that she had to make a constructive effort to improve interactions in the family; otherwise both children would be removed from the home.

The family was referred to The Family House, where the mother received individual therapy as well as group therapy in combination with twice-weekly relational work in the home where the psychotherapist from The Family House headed an intense process to address relations between parents and children. Every three months, The Family House holds a meeting for everyone involved in a case. In this case, the class teacher from Noah's reception class and the educator from his after-school programme were invited to a meeting, where the mother described how things were at home, and the reception class teacher said that she was not sure whether Noah was ready to start school after the summer holidays along with his mates. She said that Noah was very disruptive, that he was unable to follow instructions given to the whole class, that he was often late, and that conflicts with other students were a daily occurrence. He had difficulty settling down and often left the school in anger, so that the teacher had to call Noah's mother. Noah also often missed school entirely.

At the meeting, the psychotherapist from The Family House informed the participants about the treatment plan that had been drawn up in cooperation with the mother. They had decided that Noah should receive therapy based on the method of infant therapy, where specific experiences in connection with the parents' fights in the home would be verbalised. The therapeutic message was prepared, and Noah arrived for the first therapy session together with his mother. Noah listened attentively when he heard about the specific experiences he had had when he was very young. Noah became pensive and subsequently processed what we had talked about in Sandplay therapy. In the sandbox he showed that he missed his father, whom he looked up to, but also showed his anger at being abandoned.

After the therapy session, Noah's mother gave Noah's reception class teacher a copy of the day's message so that he could support Noah in relation to what he had heard during the first therapy session. Every day, both the mother and the reception class teacher wrote down any noteworthy developments. After three therapy sessions, Noah began to calm down at home. Alongside Noah's therapy the relations in the home were the subject of intense work, and a special effort was devoted to restoring the mother's contact with Ida. Noah's mother worked closely with the therapist on being with her children in a constructive way and being able to see and meet their needs. This work involved the Marte Meo method. Noah's mother did not believe that it would be possible to reach Noah, but she soon became aware that she shared a big part of the responsibility for Noah's decision to shut off contact. With a persistent effort, she was able to show Noah that there are other ways of being together than the style of interaction that had been practised in the home until then.

Noah continued in therapy and looked forward to the sessions. His conflicts with his mother became less intense, and they were able to share more and more good times. In his reception class they saw an improvement in Noah's ability to focus. They saw that he was calmer, and that he had fewer conflicts with the other children. The therapy continued during the summer holiday, and the first day of school drew near. Noah had improved considerably, and the doubts about whether he would be ready to transition to the next level had dissipated. Everyone was confident that with support from the teacher, who had been involved in the process, Noah would do fine. For Noah, starting first grade was a good experience. Once he calmed down he did well in several of his school subjects. He made friends in school and often brought friends home.

In a positive collaboration that involved Noah's mother, the school, the after-school programme and The Family House Noah was able to get in touch with himself and to enter a positive path. Ida's contact gradually improved. Infant therapy was arranged for Ida, and once it was completed she did well. She began to engage others on her own initiative and thrived in her nursery class. The mother began to notice her little girl and is now able to provide the contact she needs. Ida has developed a secure attachment to her mother.

A psychologist or a psychotherapist may reach back to a time before the child was born, before the trauma occurred, and work with the trauma, reaching back to a peaceful moment in the child's life and working through the trauma. That requires persistent cooperation with the child's parents or, if that is not possible, with the persons who care for the child instead of the parents. When professionals who are not trained therapists wish to use the method of infant therapy they address the here-and-now situations, as described in the examples mentioned above. Here, supervision plays an important supportive role.

CHAPTER FOURTEEN

Infant therapy with adopted children

Adoption as loss

Sarah was a happy, well-adjusted seventeen-year-old girl who had been adopted as an infant. She had always known that she had been adopted and had always felt at home and loved in her adoptive family. Nevertheless, she felt an undefinable sense of loss, a feeling that we have heard voiced by many other adoptees whom we have met through our work and privately. "Sometimes I feel incomplete", Sarah told us. "I need to know more: Why did it happen? What is she like? Who is my birth father? What is he like? The older I get, the more important it is to know. It's pretty frustrating being an adoptee sometimes" (Brodzinsky, Schechter & Henig, 1993, p. 11) .

There is nothing abnormal or surprising about Sarah's sense of frustration. Her feelings can be largely attributed to a sense of mourning over the parents who are so often in her thoughts. We see the same basic sense of grief in most adoptees who, like Sarah, have reached a difficult phase in their psychological development. We think that many of the aspects that have been characterised as pathological in the behaviour of adoptees is in fact a manifestation of an unacknowledged adaptive grieving process. This view has found widespread acceptance as

145

an explanation of the difficulties that children adopted above the age of one year often face later in life. Children who have had the time to develop an attachment to their initial caregivers, whether these are the birth parents, other relatives, or foster parents, before they are removed from them and placed in a new home are almost bound to experience this separation as a loss and grieve over it.

Grief almost always follows a loss and finds a wide range of emotional expressions: shock, anger, depression, despair, helplessness, hopelessness. The grief may be blocked, and it may be prolonged, but usually it is a normal reaction to the loss and serves an adaptive purpose. In late adoptions, the loss may be traumatic and a severe psychological strain for the child. However, children who are adopted at birth also suffer a loss. It is less traumatic and less manifest, but it may still have a profound impact on the child's personality. Someone who was only a few days old when the adoption took place not only mourns the loss of the birth parents they never had a chance to know; they also mourn other aspects of themselves, which they lost in the adoption: the loss of their roots, of family continuity, of a self-image without "blank spots". They may also lose faith in their relationship with the adoptive parents as permanent and enduring. If the first parents could give them up, why not the next set?

With early adoptees, the loss is usually not acute or traumatic, and the child is rarely aware of it before the age of five years. The awareness emerges gradually with the child's growing cognitive understanding of what it means to be adopted. That can lead to behavioural changes in childhood that may not initially appear to have anything to do with loss and grief.

Sometimes the grief becomes a key factor in the adoptee's life; sometimes it does not. Some adoptees are seized by an overwhelming sense of alienation and disconnectedness. Others, for reasons that may be hard to explain, avoid such feelings and are instead deeply grateful for having been raised in the safe and loving home that their adoptive parents provided for them.

We cannot predict which adoptees will feel incomplete or abandoned, and who will feel gratitude; who will focus on the "loss" of adoption, and who will dwell only on what they "gained". However, we can say that both reaction patterns are understandable and common, and that they may occur in the same individual at different times in the person's life.

Using the method of infant therapy with adopted children poses a particular challenge for the therapist, because our knowledge about the child's life prior to the adoption is always fraught with gaps, inaccuracies, and a degree of general uncertainty. Since the therapist only tells the child what is true, preparing for the therapy takes some skill. The new parents' meeting with the child forms the point of departure for the therapy, regardless of the child's age, and regardless whether this meeting took place in a residential institution, at a hospital, or in a foster family in the child's native country. At this point we have knowledge that we know is true. However, we also know that the child has been separated from people that she was associated with, and we know what such a separation can mean for a young child. What we do not know is what it meant for this particular child. For these reasons, we always meet this group of children with a natural sense of humility.

Case: Anna

Anna's parents contacted my (IP) private clinic when Anna was just over four years old. At the age of three months, she had been picked up by her adoptive parents from an orphanage in South America.

The reason for the adoptive parents' request for a consultation was deep concern for Anna's development, especially with regard to attachment. The parents worried that Anna might have autism. Occasionally, she would bang her head against the floor, and she engaged in monotonous rocking. Her language skills were poor, and she was a very restless child. Anna could not stay calm, even for short intervals of time. She was active all the time, with no particular focus. She "fluttered" around aimlessly. The parents found Anna difficult to engage, and they had had her hearing tested repeatedly but were told that there was nothing wrong. It was becoming increasingly difficult for the parents to contact Anna; she also preferred to avoid physical contact. She had trouble falling asleep at night, even when she was very tired.

What we know is that she was dropped off at the orphanage shortly after her birth, and that she fell ill a few months later and had to go to hospital. In hospital, she was on her own. Shortly after her stay in hospital, which lasted a week, she was introduced to her adoptive parents at the orphanage.

The aspects I choose to focus on are her separation from her birth mother and her life at the orphanage with many other children and few adults, which presents difficult conditions for attachment. Anna fell ill. She was hospitalised on her own. We presume that Anna was subjected to examinations and thus to pain and discomfort which she may have had to handle without help from anyone, her only means of defence being to withdraw from the outside world.

During the first therapy session, Anna listens but remains passive and unresponsive to what I tell her about the first part of her life. After the therapy session she works in the sandboxes, where she actively sets to work while I act as her tacit, acknowledging witness. On several occasions, Anna stops her activity and holds my gaze for a long time with her big, deep eyes in intense present moments. I ask Anna to pay a symbolic fee. Before each therapy session, Anna pays a symbolic fee of a pebble. The arrangement is that if she does not want to hear what I have to tell her, she will show up without a pebble. In that case I will speak to her parents instead.

When Anna comes in for the second therapy session she does not bring a pebble, but she clearly listens attentively to what I told the parents about Anna's early life. On several occasions she looks at me with an investigative gaze, this time coupled with a sullen and dismissive attitude.

For the third therapy session Anna enters the therapy room with her hand held out, and in her hand she has a pebble that she immediately pays me. Then Anna finds her seat, sits down and looks at me with a reserved but expectant look. I tell her about her time in the hospital, about being on her own, and I sense a rare quality of intensity in our contact and note important moments of meeting.

After the three therapy sessions there is significant progress in Anna's attachment and in her development in general. After the therapy, teachers from Anna's preschool said that she was a quiet and harmonious girl who was at ease with herself, and in the home, the parents noticed that Anna had achieved a sense of inner calm. She was now able to sit on her own with a book, and she also enjoyed having someone read her a story. When the parents read aloud to her, Anna sought close bodily contact with her parents. At night, when Anna got her goodnight hug, she insisted on a close and warm hug. If she did not feel that the parents were sufficiently focused in their presence, she would demand a proper hug. If Anna wanted a hug during the day she would climb up on a stool or a chair to make sure the embrace was sufficiently warm and intense. Anna's language gradually became age-appropriate. When she began in therapy she had begun to take lessons from a speech therapist in her preschool, but suddenly she progressed rapidly. Anna's rocking stopped, and she also stopped banging her head against the floor. She generally sleeps well at night now, and when she has trouble falling asleep she relaxes in her bed.

Three years after the therapy, Anna's parents have no doubt that the therapy helped their daughter. Prior to therapy, Anna had difficulty accepting care, and now the parents see a loving girl who believes in herself and, not least, in life. Anna has found inner peace.

The assessment from her school now is that "Anna is a girl at ease with herself. She is good at focusing, and she is never in any doubt about what to do when we give instructions to the group. Anna is a harmonious girl who remembers to be considerate of the other children. She is a girl with a lot to offer".

Therapeutic reflections

Among my considerations prior to the therapy—in relation to Anna as an adopted child—was Dolto's thoughts about a child's sudden separation from his or her mother; the mother and the body that the child lived in and was surrounded by. A newborn baby has the same identity as his or her mother right after birth, so apart from the warm body she had known for nine months, Anna also lost her identity. That is why this "disruption" was so important to convey to her. We know that the conditions for attachment in a South American orphanage may be fraught with challenges for a young child. Therefore we assume that Anna did not receive the fundamental sense of security that might have helped her grow strong. Anna fell ill, was hospitalised, and was on her own. There is a high probability that she felt abandoned.

The language barrier may be traced back to the traumatic situation Anna found herself in. We know that "the body remembers", and that early traumas may block the development of essential functions, in this case language. By putting the child's trauma into words, we dissolve the blockage, and the child develops the ability to speak.

Anna's life related to Per Schultz Jørgensen's model

Anna is a *vulnerable* child. At the age of four years, she rejects close physical contact. She self-harms and is restless and unfocused. She has language difficulties and sleep problems. She cannot play on her own, and she is constantly restless. Anna has experienced many stressful situations. At an early age she was separated from her biological mother and placed in in orphanage in South America. She was hospitalised on her own. She did not receive optimal care or had the opportunity to establish an attachment relationship. The consequences are inadequate identity development, post-traumatic stress syndrome (PTSD) as a result of early traumas, language difficulties, and a dissociative defence. The protective factors in Anna's life are the adoptive parents, her new family, life in preschool, and the treatment she receives based on the method of infant therapy. The protection that Anna receives makes her less vulnerable, as she develops resilience along with developing her identity, language, and attachment. As a consequence, Anna is now on a convincing and healthy development path.

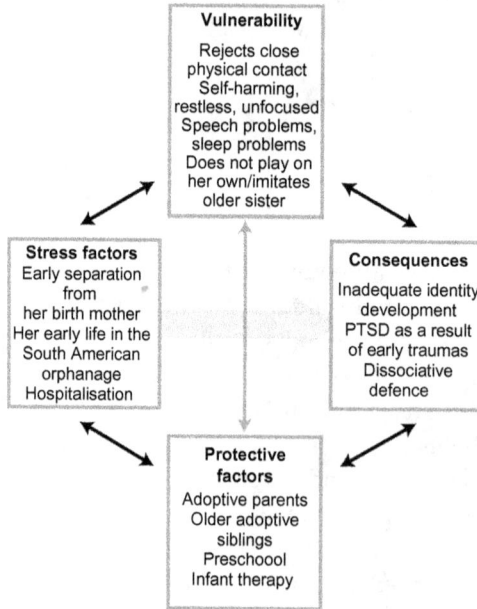

Vulnerability

Rejects close
physical contact
Self-harming,
restless, unfocused
Speech problems,
sleep problems
Does not play on
her own/imitates
older sister

Stress factors

Early separation
from
her birth mother
Her early life in the
South American
orphanage
Hospitalisation

Consequences

Inadequate identity
development
PTSD as a result
of early traumas
Dissociative
defence

**Protective
factors**

Adoptive parents
Older adoptive
siblings
Preschoool
Infant therapy

Figure 2. Model of the interaction between stress factors and risk factors (Source: Jørgensen, Ertmann, Egelund, & Hermann, 1993, p. 175).

CHAPTER FIFTEEN

The method of infant therapy in adult therapy

Therapy with adults who have experienced early trauma

As therapists we often meet adults who have a hard life and limited will to live. They present diffuse symptoms. They talk about anxiety, restlessness, and concentration problems. Often, they have experienced traumas before they acquired language.

An example

A thirty-year-old father said that he had been delivered one month pre-term by a caesarean section. The doctors had noticed that he had stopped gaining weight, so they decided for a caesarean. When he was born they found that the umbilical cord was wrapped around his neck, and that he had suffered hypoxia. As an adult he had a recurring sensation of not being able to breathe. He now suffered from panic attacks, was unable to go into stores, walk down the street, or be in crowded places. He received treatment, in part based on the method of infant therapy, and his early experiences were put into words. He felt a sense of release and gradually experienced positive changes accompanied by a significant reduction in symptoms.

151

When we hear or read a patient history and notice that a person has experienced traumatic situations before acquiring language, and we see that the person is struggling with issues that may be rooted in early trauma, we offer therapy based on the method of infant therapy, often with a course of three therapy sessions. With the client we talk about the specific incidents that occurred. We ask about the pregnancy and the delivery, about any separations from the parents and other caregivers and about health problems and hospitalisations. The separation from the mother, with whom the child was so intimately connected for nine months, is often stressful for the newborn child.

We ask about family secrets, which are often troubling for the children in the family. If a child finds his mother lifeless in the bathtub in blood-red water and later hears the father tell the family that the mother passed away peacefully in her sleep after a stroke, the child faces a dilemma. In this case, the boy, who had a very different image of what happened, was dismissed when he told his father what he had seen. The father stuck to his story. He looked overbearingly at his son and said that he appeared to have a rather over-active imagination. Since that day it was difficult for the boy to have faith in the accuracy of his own perceptions.

We also ask whether the person resembles any other family members. Children can often become carriers of their parents' projections. An eight-year-old boy looked like his grandfather, whom his mother disliked intensely. When the mother told the boy that she did not feel acknowledged when she was with the grandfather, and that he looked like the grandfather, walked in the same way, and spoke the same dialect, the boy understood that his mother was not upset with him but in fact felt put down when she saw her own father in her son.

These are the specific incidents we ask about, and those are the ones that the therapist later, in a therapeutic context, tells to the client. The therapist sticks to the specifics that the client has described. Often, the client describes very difficult experiences without being emotionally affected by them. When the therapist empathises with the young child's experience of the same incidents, for example being abandoned by her mother and subsequently placed in an orphanage, the client is "seen". The body remembers, and here, the emotions are associated with the aspect that was cleaved off and tied up energy. Many clients who have been in this type of therapy say that their life has taken on more nuances, and that they feel liberated and more alive.

It can be a challenge for an adult to remember what it was like. However, we all carry our history with us. What we went through and the way we perceived the world continue to influence our life today. In preparing the therapy we ask what sort of family the client was born into. What the home looked like, where the client's bed was, and what sort of atmosphere prevailed in the home. How emotions were shared, and whether it was even allowed to express emotions. Was there anyone that the client had a particular sense of sympathy for or attachment with?

The clients are encouraged to contact the parents or others who knew them when they were infants or children, to hear what they might remember from that time. Based on this talk with the client, the therapist considers which specific incidents it will be essential to put into words. In therapy, the therapist asks the client to listen while the therapist tells what happened, and what the therapist thinks the experience must have been like for the client at such a young age.

Therapy with parents and their grown children

Sometimes we receive requests from parents with grown children who have faced difficulties throughout their lives due to traumatic experiences, for example in connection with a divorce or conflicts between parents. The parents keep blaming themselves for what happened. After conversations with the parents we plan the therapy sessions, and then the parents come in together with their child, who is now an adult, and we put the specific experiences into words. Next, we work in the sandboxes. The grown children are asked to work with symbols in the sandbox and to answer the question, "What is your experience of your early life with your parents?" The parents are asked, "What is your experience of your child's early life with you?" When they have represented the individual experiences via the symbols in the sand, they talk about them. Later, each of them makes a sand representation using the symbols, to illustrate what sort of future they would like to see.

Grown children and their parents have told us that it felt very liberating when the unsaid was put into words. Because the difficult things were spoken they can now refer to the therapy and thus the difficult experiences that are now no longer taboo, thanks to the therapy process. Often, what the parents thought was stressful for their adult child only exists in the parents' perception. For the grown child, the difficulties may stem from other sources entirely.

Case: Kent. Therapy with a grown man

Sixty-six-year-old Kent contacted me (IT) after hearing about our work at Skodsborg with eating disorders in young children born with drug withdrawal and early damage due to the mother's use of alcohol during pregnancy. The children received infant therapy. "Can you ever be too old for that?" he asked. The answer was no. It was one of Dolto's key points that anyone, regardless of age and other factors, can benefit from this therapy form.

Kent's story

Kent had eating problems. Four months earlier he had been diagnosed with cancer of the oesophagus and undergone two major surgical procedures. Most of his oesophagus had been removed, and his stomach had been relocated to a place underneath one side of his collar bone. Septicaemia had set in and almost killed him. Kent survived, and he was relieved to have left all that behind him. But here he was, now, with a tube running into his nose and liquid nourishment in a plastic bag hanging from a rack next to his chair. In the hospital ward they said that he was being hysterical when he was unable to eat the food they served him. After two conversations, the therapy began.

"You are a proud man who has come far in life. You are used to sitting at the head of the table and presiding over important meetings. Now you feel small and humbled. It bothers you that the staff in the hospital have called you 'hysterical'. The staff has observed your suffering, everything that you've gone through. And yet, they call you hysterical.

You want help to be able to eat. You are motivated to make an effort. I think that it's natural to have difficulty eating after the experiences have had. You have had a lot of different objects inside your mouth. You were on a respirator for several days, and you had general anaesthesia. The lining in your throat and mouth are sore and sensitive. I think that your throat must have hurt, and that you have had trouble swallowing.

Due to these experiences we need to make a plan to help you regain your ability to enjoy eating again. I am sure that we will succeed. You have overcome a difficult period of ill health. You will get through this too. I am going to help you".

After this initial therapy session, Kent and I spoke. We spoke about his childhood. I interviewed Kent about meals he remembered from his childhood. What did his mother or his grandmother make for him? The garden in his childhood home was full of fruit trees and berry bushes, and fruit was a part of most meals, especially in the summer. Freshly made apple sauce was delicious—apple sauce made of the right kinds of apples, which can be hard to come by today. "Belle de Boskoop—that's a traditional cooking apple, the skin is thick, and it's not an apple you'd want to sink your teeth into, but the flavour when it's cooked the way my mother did: heavenly!" Kent smiled. Apple sauce on barley porridge. Nice!

Stewed fruit was another favourite dish. Stewed fruit with cream and a sprinkling of sugar. Just a touch. As a boy, Kent loved pureed stewed strawberries, where the berries themselves had been removed. The deep red syrup was wonderful. "In the morning, we had junket that had set overnight. We sprinkled it with soft brown sugar". In Kent's mind, he watched the images of his childhood, like a film. The house, the garden, the loving care, a glass of juice in the tree house brought up via the rope ladder through the secret entrance. His mother calling him from the garden door, when it was time for dinner. Kent had nice, warm memories. And we dwelled on those.

Kent's wife, Birgit, was included as a natural part of the plan we had made. She was going to find the right apples, cook apple sauce to the best of her abilities, prepare barley porridge with the right texture, neither stodgy nor runny, and she would serve the dishes in little bowls, everything separately. Just a single meal before the next therapy session would constitute a success.

We did a total of seven therapy sessions, at one-week intervals. During the first week, Kent had barley porridge with apple sauce twice, and he had enjoyed it. Every therapy session followed the same pattern, except that I would expand the pattern by articulating his latest success.

"You have now told me that you have had barley porridge with apple sauce. You have had new experiences. You are a strong person. I know that you are going to make it. You have already overcome severe stress factors".

The process continued. Kent visualised experiences with food from throughout his life. He recalled flavour experiences from big dinners and from picnics with plain sandwiches, from trips abroad and everyday simple meals in the summer house. The sensation of having food in his mouth, of the food when it touches the tongue, the palate, and the throat, was especially important. The food had to have a soft texture.

After the second therapy session, Kent had stewed pureed strawberries where the berries had been removed. Later he had mashed potatoes with meat sauce, then lasagne and moussaka, and other soft-textured dishes followed. Citrus fruits were squeezed and pureed, and less and less of his food came through a tube. After seven weeks and seven therapy sessions, Kent rang me and said that he had had his first steak, and that he had enjoyed it.

In my therapy with Kent I used the method of infant therapy to provide a general structure that I used every time, seven times in total. The structure of infant therapy helped me maintain my authority as a therapist in a process that, in addition to the therapy itself, included visualisation, informal dialogues, and meal plans. Throughout the course of my therapy with Kent I often thought of a particular boy, Martin, who had been born with foetal alcohol syndrome, and who had had trouble eating, both as a young boy, as an older boy, and as an adolescent. Martin's difficulties were caused by his mother's alcohol abuse during pregnancy. From my work with him I knew that it takes the controlled coordination of eight different muscle groups, from the food passes between the lips until it is swallowed and goes down the throat. I learned that people who have difficulty eating need to be treated with gentle care and respect. This experience was useful for me when I met Kent.

CHAPTER SIXTEEN

National and international interest in identifying and treating trauma in infants

This book deals with a treatment approach that is mainly aimed at children aged nought to three years, although the method can also, as described, be applied with older children, adolescents, and adults.

In recent years we have seen an increased focus on infants and on the potential impact of traumatic experiences early in life on the child's short-term and long-term development. We are convinced that infant therapy has the capacity to help many children with early traumas, and that additional research in this field is crucial.

International studies of the occurrence and impact of trauma exposure

There is very limited knowledge about the extent to which children are affected by traumatic and stressful experiences. A widespread theory has been that very young children are less affected by these experiences than older children and adults because they are too young to grasp the gravity of what is happening and to put their experiences into words. Recent research (Margolin & Vickerman, 2011) has found, however, that even infants are affected much more by traumatic experiences than previously assumed, and that these experiences may have severe and life-long psychological consequences. On this background, the assessment and identification of infant traumas has become a new focus area, also in an international context.

We know that children often react differently than adults to potentially traumatic situations (Scheeringa & Zeanah, 2001). Children's way of handling a trauma depends very much on the support they receive from their environment, especially from their close family. Many studies have documented the importance of including the relational perspective when assessing children's reactions to traumatic events (ibid). This means that we should include the parents in the assessment of children's symptoms after traumatic experiences, and that it is essential to teach the parents how best to support their child.

Recent research has shown that being exposed to trauma early in life may affect the child's biological, emotional, social, and cognitive functioning in both the short term and the long term (Chu & Lieberman, 2010). Exposure to early trauma has also been found to constitute a risk factor for developing psychological disorders such as post-traumatic stress disorder (PTSD) (Elklit & Gudmunsdottir, 2006), anxiety and depression, substance abuse, eating disorders, and general ill health later in life.

Many children who have been exposed to traumatic experiences are not identified and are therefore not offered any treatment. In the Danish debate, several explanations have been suggested as to why the children are not identified. One explanation may be that childcare professionals and educators have insufficient knowledge about how children might react after being exposed to a traumatic incident. Another possible explanation is that these professionals lack validated tools in Danish for identifying especially the youngest children/infants.

American studies have found that many children are exposed to potentially traumatic incidents, and that children often develop PTSD symptoms due to these experiences. In a sample of 1,420 American children, sixty-eight per cent were found to have experienced at least one potentially traumatic incident, and thirty-seven per cent had experienced two or more (Scheeringa, Zeanah, & Cohen, 2011). A wide range of experiences, including violence, sexual abuse, fires, natural disasters, hospitalisation, and traffic accidents, may lead to PTSD symptoms in children. Both in Denmark and around the world, there is a growing focus on hospitalisation of young children and infants. About one fourth of the children who have been in a intensive care unit show negative psychological consequences from their hospital stay. These children are at risk of developing PTSD.

Research has also found that recurring experiences of pain in infants may have an adverse effect on the child's neurological development. Painful and stressful experiences are normal for newborn children (blood tests, suction, IV infusions, infections, etc.), but research has found that recurring pain experiences can lead to cortical and hippocampal cell death, which in the long term may lead to changes in pain perception, learning, and attention functions in infants and young children. Furthermore, recurring pain may also lead to an increased vulnerability to stress, anxiety and, in the long term, other mental health problems (Anand, 2000).

Multiple studies have found that once a child has developed PTSD symptoms, these symptoms are often fairly chronic in character, and that these children often display symptoms several years after the traumatic experiences. That is why The American Academy of Child & Adolescent Psychiatry recommends that all psychiatric and psychological assessments of children should routinely include questions about exposure to traumatic incidents and PTSD symptoms. This screening should be performed using validated and developmentally sensitive instruments. If a screening indicates significant PTSD symptoms the child should undergo further PTSD testing to assess the severity and duration of the symptoms and whether the child's daily functioning is affected.

Trauma prevention

Hospitalisation

Hospital stays and visits for infants and young children are recurring causes of traumatisation. Our knowledge about this is steadily growing, but there is a big gap between knowledge and practice. Currently, there is widespread knowledge that certain measures, for example having the parents by the child's side during painful procedures, can lessen the child's pain and discomfort, but it can be difficult for healthcare professionals without psychological training to prioritise this due to time pressures and other concerns.

We lack instruments for acquiring evidence-based knowledge in this area. We need a specific hospital scale, as someone who is not familiar with the hospital environment and hospital procedures will have difficulty asking the right questions and interpreting the child's signals correctly. We also need instruments for measuring and assessing whether the parents are offering the child the right form of help and support, and we need screening instruments for quickly assessing whether the attachment patterns give cause for concern, both in relation to children who are traumatised by the hospital stay/visit and in relation to children who are traumatised for other reasons.

At Skodsborg, we have always made deliberate efforts to prevent traumatic effects of hospital visits or stays. We see it as our responsibility to protect the children staying at Skodsborg. The goal was to give the children the best possible protection from any kind of abuse, from loss of any kind, and from anxiety-provoking experiences that risked undermining the trust that may have only recently been achieved in relation to the contact person. Remarkably, this protection is hardest to ensure in the collaboration with doctors and other hospital staff, which means that follow-up visits to the hospital are often associated with experiences that transgress both psychological and physical boundaries. Therefore, we usually have at least two members of staff or one parent and a staff member go along for these visits, so that one person can focus fully on taking care of the child, while the other conveys information about the child to the hospital staff.

The point is to prevent "our" child from having adverse reactions to a procedure for several days after the visit. Therefore the child should mainly be handled by familiar hands; for example, the mother or the contact person should be the one to undress the child. The child should not have to be naked, since that is not required for any examination. The child should not be placed on paper or cold plastic but should lie on her own duvet/blanket, and the child should not have bright light shining right in her face.

The child should not be touched by cold hands or instruments. We also emphasise that no one who is a stranger to the child should ever touch the child until after the child has been told what is going to happen This also applies to infants. Loud voices and noises should be minimised, as should the number of people standing around the child. Examinations should take place in a calm place, without doors opening and closing, people hurrying back and forth or beeping pagers. If it is necessary to use a needle, the skin should be numbed first with a local anaesthetic ointment or spray. The doctor attached to Skodsborg always does it this way, and all the older children in the house are familiar with the doctor's "magic ointment". In addition, the doctor should attribute great importance to information from the child's contact person to ensure a nuanced dialogue about the individual child between two professionals or between the doctor and the child's parents.

These features are important for all children, but they are especially crucial for children who have suffered neglect or abuse, who may have just recently left their home and have not yet settled into a new place and become familiar with the new people there. An important part of the treatment is to supplement the child's often meagre collection of good experiences that support his personality development. For a fragile infant undergoing withdrawal, a medical examination can stop the ongoing development or send the child straight into sustained relapse. With these children, we have often suggested that the hospital physician who wanted to see the child should come to Skodsborg in order to perform the examination in the child's familiar surroundings. If it is necessary to hospitalise a child, a familiar adult or the child's parents will be with the child at all times, so that the child is never alone.

Removing a child from the home

Placing a child in a residential institution or in a foster family is another area that involves a high risk of traumatisation. Often, the child's parents are not able to support their child, and the professionals who might support the child often lack sufficient knowledge or approach the task in an urgent and inadequate manner. The child is left, with his pain, in an unfamiliar environment surrounded by unfamiliar adults. The professionals may be so appalled by what they see in the home that their actions are guided by this impression and their emotional response rather than by their knowledge about what is important to a young child in crisis.

Many parents speak to their child just after birth and continue to do so as the child grows up. They use words to describe the many things happening in the course of day. Nursery and preschool staff also speak to the children in their care, and professional caregivers place a high priority on the little dialogues between child and adult that help the child learn about the world. This often changes when the adult is under pressure, and serious topics are on the agenda. There is a tendency to "forget" that infants too need to be updated about what is happening, for example when they are picked up by strangers and taken to an unfamiliar place.

The adult has to verbalise what is happening. The child needs to be told what is going on. Who has decided it, and what consequences is it going to have? Here, social workers can use methods from infant therapy to put life into words, as it is right now. Dolto found that even very young children are soothed and relieved when they hear about the reality they are living. Caregivers can use the method of infant therapy in here-and-now situations. Thormann and Guldberg (2011) relate the case of two young boys, Matt and Martin, who were removed from their mother without being told anything. They were torn from their mother's arms while she was held back by two police officers. When the taxi with the children and the social worker arrived at Skodsborg, the caregiver who met the children asked what they had been told. The social worker said that no one had told them anything, since they were so young (two and four years, respectively). In Matt and Martin's case, the social worker could have talked to the children and used the method of infant therapy, for example saying,

> "Hi. My name is Linda. I am a social worker. I know your mummy. It has been decided that you need to live somewhere else for some time. Your mummy cannot look after you at home. The place you are going to live is called Skodsborg. Skodsborg is a home for children. Your mummy is very upset, and she is angry about the decision that has been made. That is why she didn't want to open the door, and she didn't want to help us pack some things for you. I am going to talk to her, and I hope that we can both visit you tomorrow. We'll bring your clothes and your toys. Your mummy knows where you are going to live. She has the address and the phone number. Come, we're going to Skodsborg now".

Once the children had arrived at Skodsborg, Linda could have repeated what she said earlier, so that the caregiver who met the children heard it and knew what the children had been told. With this simple measure, Matt and Martin could have been treated decently and with respect, even at their young age. If it proved possible to arrange for the mother and the social worker to visit the following day, bringing toys and clothes, the situation would have come full circle. The mother would see where the children are going to stay, put their clothes in the closet and sit down with the caregiver for a cup of coffee. Saying and doing what is described here is not difficult, per se, but it requires the understanding that this is part of providing proper care for the child. Social workers need to be introduced to the method and grasp the importance of this approach to be able to use it in high-pressure emergency situations.

Hospitalisations and placements outside the home are recurring experiences for many children. Having an explicitly stated procedure facilitates the situation. The responsible adults are prepared to deal with the situation, because they are familiar with the given frame of reference, and that has been the case for many years at Skodsborg. No member of staff has had any doubt about the guidelines that apply in these recurring situations. The same procedures could be introduced in Social Services/Child Protective Services. This would help to prevent trauma and therefore constitutes a crucial part of the practice.

In connection with both hospitalisations and placements outside the home, trauma prevention involves preserving the crucial sense of continuity in the child's life. This is facilitated when the child receives personal support from close caregivers and professionals, from spoken words, and from having her personal belongings within reach. The personal belongings act as transitional objects. Along with the words that verbalise the child's situation, these elements are crucial protective factors for the child.

Inspiration from additional infant research

Among the more recent research, we have found Professor Sam Tyano's research at the Tel Aviv University, Sackler School of Medicine about the development of PTSD in early childhood especially inspiring. At a lecture he gave at the University of Southern Denmark in spring 2012, he highlighted some key guidelines that everyone working with infants and young children should be aware of, regardless of the nature of the traumatic incident the child has been exposed to:

- Never assume that the child is too young to understand;
- Identify stress factors and protective factors for the development of PTSD;
- Assess whether intervention is needed, and;

- If intervention is needed, both the child and the attachment figure should be present in the therapy room.

Risk factors for the development of PTSD
in infants and young children

- The most powerful trauma variable to predict the development of PTSD in infants and young children is not an incident directed at them personally but witnessing a threat against a close attachment figure;
- Children who were older than eighteen months when they were exposed to an acute trauma develop more flashback symptoms than younger children;
- Having a father who suffers from PTSD;
- Having a mother who has inner representations of herself as a protective mother without actually being a protective mother;
- Generally poor family conditions;
- Girls are more at risk, and the risk is greater the younger the girl is;
- Difficult/problematic temperament.

Protective factors in relation to the development
of PTSD in infants and young children

- Positive relations between the parents;
- Parents who have constructive coping strategies;
- Close physical contact between and parents;
- Social supports;
- Support from society.

Sam Tyano also spoke of his work with "dyadic psychotherapy", which aims to:

- Integrate the fragmented, traumatic memory;
- Strengthen the mother's confidence to empower her to serve as a protective shield for the child;
- Restore the child's capacity for symbolic play and exploration;
- Introduce the possibility of restoring the concept/representation of, for example, the abusive parent (Keren & Tyano, 2009).

This approach is quite similar to the method of infant therapy, as it has evolved in Denmark, which includes the parents or, in their absence, the child's caregiver. The adult caregiver, the parents, or a teacher will be involved in the therapy as a form of co-therapist. In working with older children, we use infant therapy combined with play therapy and activities with clay, drawings, or Sandplay, where the child has an opportunity to reconstruct the trauma via creative activity and play.

Danish initiatives

In recent years, several dramatic cases of atrocious abuse and neglect have again raised the question of why these situations are allowed to exist, and why authorities have not intervened much earlier. However, there is no systematic method in place today for identifying children under five years of age who are exposed to experiences that are so traumatic that the child needs help.

Professor Ask Elklit from the National Center of Psychotraumatology at the University of Southern Denmark has taken the initiative to develop a systematic method for identifying young who have suffered psychological damage from abuse, neglect, illness, or accidents. In Denmark, two per cent of all children, that is 1,200 children a year, are victims of sexual abuse. Another 2.1% suffer neglect, physical abuse or systematic devaluation (Christoffersen, 2010). The test is intended to cover a wide range of situations, for example also to determine whether a child has severe psychological after-effects from accidents, abuse, or lengthy hospital stays. It is easy to check whether a child has physical injuries, for example in an X-ray. Mental injuries are much harder to spot, because children respond very differently to traumatic experiences. Some become very aggressive, for no apparent reason, while others stop playing, withdraw, and make sure not to be any trouble. We are delighted to see these positive developments in our own country. Another major challenge is to find ways to document the efficacy of infant therapy and the methods it involves, using evidence-based findings.

REFERENCES

Anand, K. J. (2000). Effects of perinatal pain and stress. *Progress in Brain Research, 122*: 117–129.

Bowlby, J. (1940). The influence of early environment in the development of neurosis and neurotic character. *International Journal of Psycho-Analysis, 21*: 154–178.

Bowlby, J. (1969). *Attachment and Loss. Vol. 1: Attachment*. Middlesex: Penguin Press.

Bowlby, J. (1973). *Attachment and Loss. Vol. 2: Separation, Anxiety and Anger*. London: Hogarth Press.

Brazelton, T. B. (1984). *Neonatal Behavioral Assessment Scale. 2nd edition*. Oxford: Blackwell Scientific Publications.

Brazelton, T. B., & Nugent, J. K. (1994). *Neonatal Behavioral Assessment Scale. 3rd edition*. Cambridge: Cambridge University Press.

Brodzinsky, D. M., Schechter, M. D., & Henig, R. M. (1993). *Being Adopted. The Lifelong Search for Self*. New York, NY: Anchor Books.

Christoffersen, M. N. (2010). *Børnemishandling i hjemmet*. SFI rapport 10/30. Copenhagen: SFI—The Danish National Centre for Social Research.

Chu, A. T., & Lieberman, A. F. (2010). Clinical implications of traumatic stress from birth to age five. *Annual Review of Clinical Psychology, 6*: 469–494.

Dolto, F. (1988). *Samtaler om børn og psykoanalyse*. Copenhagen: Hans Reitzels Forlag. [Original French edition (1985): *Seminaire de psychanalyse d'enfants*. Paris: coop. Jean-François de Sauverzac.]

Dolto, F. (1993). *För barnets skull*. Stockholm: Nordstedts Förlag. [Original French edition (1985): *La cause des enfants*. Paris: Robert Laffont.]

Dolto, F. (1998). *Fallet Dominique*. Stockholm: Rabén Prisma. [Original French edition (1974): Le cas Dominique. Paris: Seuil. English edition: Dolto, F. (1974). *Dominique: Analysis of an Adolescent*. London: Souvenir Press.]

Eliacheff, C. (1994). *Krop og skrig. Psykoanalytiker blandt spædbørn*. Copenhagen: Borgens Forlag. [Original French edition (1993): *À corps et à cris, être psychanalyste avec les tout petits*. Paris: Odile Jacob.]

Elklit, A., & Gudmunsdottir, D. (2006). *Posttraumatisk stressforstyrrelse hos børn og unge*. Den blå serie. B29. Herfølge: Forlaget Skolepsykologi.

Fraiberg, S. (1980). *The Magic Years. Understanding and Handling the Problems of Early Childhood*. New York, NY: Charles Scribner's Sons, Inc.

Gautré-Delay, F. (2000). *Sprogbrug og praksis ved fjernelse af spædbørn— en pilotundersøgelse*. Agrippa, 20: 72–89.

Goldfarb, W. (1943). The effects of institutional care on adolescent personality. *Journal of Experimental Education, 119*: 661–666.

Hagemann Hansen, B., & Munck, H. (2002). *En bedre start på livet. Kortlægning og beskrivelse af 49 spædbørnsprojekter i Danmark. Forskningsrapport, no. 2*. Copenhagen: Department of Psychology. University of Copenhagen.

Hart, S. (2008). *Brain, Attachment, Personality: An Introduction to Neuroaffective Development*. London: Karnac.

Hart, S. (2009). *Den følsomme hjerne*. Copenhagen: Hans Reitzels Forlag.

Hart, S. (2011). *Neuroaffektiv psykoterapi med børn*. Copenhagen: Hans Reitzels Forlag.

Hart, S. (2011b). *The Impact of Attachment. Developmental Neuroaffective Psychology*. New York, NY: Norton.

Hart, S., & Schwartz, R. (2008). *Fra interaktion til relation*. Copenhagen: Hans Reitzels Forlag.

Heinicke, C., & Westheimer, I. (1966). *Brief Separations*. New York, NY: International Universities Press.

Jørgensen, P. S., Ertmann, B., Egelund, N., & Hermann, D. (1993). *Risikobørn. Hvem er de, hvad gør vi?* Copenhagen: Ministry of Social Affairs.

Keren, M., & Tyano, S. (2009). A developmental approach: Looking at the specificity of reactions to trauma in infants. In: D. Brom, R. Pat-Horenczyk & J. D. Ford (Eds.), *Treating Traumatized Children, Risk, Resilience and Recovery* (pp. 85–101). New York, NY: Routledge.

Lier, L. Spædbarnspsykiatri. In: T. Aarkrog, T. Isager, O. S. Jørgensen, F. W. Larsen & L. Lier (Eds.), (1999). *Børne- og ungdomspsykiatri* (pp. 495–498). Copenhagen: Hans Reitzels Forlag.

Margolin, G., & Vickerman, K. A. (2011). Posttraumatic stress in children and adolescents exposed to family violence: Overview and issues. *Couple and Family Psychology: Research and Practice, 1*: 63–73.

Marvin, R. S. (1977). An ethological-cognitive model for the attenuation of mother–child attachment behavior. In: T. Alloway, L. Krames & P. Pliner (Eds.), *Attachment Behavior*. New York, NY: Plenum.

Munck, H., & Poulsen, I. (1984). Et center for spædbørn 0–1 år og deres familier. In: P. S. Jørgensen & O. Almstrup (Eds.), *Børn og terapi. Universitetets børnepsykologiske klinik 40 år* (pp. 159–173). Copenhagen: Dansk Psykologisk Forlag.

Pascalis, O., de Schonen, S., Morton, J., Deruelle, C., & Fabre-Grenet, M. (1995). Mother's face recognition by neonates: A replication and an extension. *Infant Behaviour and Development, 18*:79–85.

Schaffer, R. (1996). *Social Development: An Introduction*. Oxford, UK/Malden, MA, USA: Blackwell Publishers.

Scheeringa, M. S., & Zeanah, C. H. (2001). A relational perspective on PTSD in early childhood. *Journal of Traumatic Stress, 4*: 799–815.

Scheeringa, M. S., Zeanah, C. H., & Cohen, J. A. (2011). PTSD in children and adolescents: towards an empirically based algorithm. *Depression and Anxiety, 9*: 770–782.

Smith, L. (2002). *Tilknytning og barns utvikling*. Kristiansand: Høyskoleforlaget.

Spitz, R. (1965). *The First Years of Life*. New York, NY: International Universities Press.

Stern, D. (1985). *The Interpersonal World of the Infant: A View from Psychoanalysis and Development*. New York, NY: Basic Books.

Stern, D. (1995). *The Motherhood Constellation: A Unified View of Parent–Infant Psychotherapy*. New York, NY: Basic Books.

Stern, D. (2004). *The Present Moment in Psychotherapy and Everyday Life*. New York, NY: Norton.

Thompson, R. A. (1999). Early attachment and later development. In: J. Cassidy & P. R. Shaver (Eds.), *Handbook of Attachment Research*. New York, NY: Guilford.

Thormann, I. (2006). *Medfødte alkoholskader. Omsorg og behandling*. Copenhagen: Hans Reitzels Forlag.

Thormann, I. (2009). *De voksne born—Om omsorgssvigt og resiliens*. Copenhagen: Hans Reitzels Forlag.

Thormann, I., Boesen, E., & Nielsen, K. (1990). *Børn i krise. En efterundersøgelse af børn fra Skodsborg Observationshjem*. Copenhagen: Skodsborg Observationshjem.

Thormann, I., & Guldberg, C. (1995). *Hånden på hjertet. Omsorg for det lille barn i krise*. Copenhagen: Hans Reitzels Forlag.

Thormann, I., & Guldberg, C. (2003). *Med Hjerte og Forstand. De tidlige anbringelser*. Copenhagen: Hans Reitzels Forlag.

Thormann, I., & Guldberg, C. (2011). *Den nænsomme anbringelse.* Copenhagen: Hans Reitzels Forlag.

Thornsohn, B. (2007). *Skæbner i skyggeland—Terapi og dæmoner.* Gjern: Hovedland.

Zacho, L. M. Sandkassen—et psykisk værksted. In: P. Skogeman, (Ed.) (2001). *Symbol, analyse, virkelighed. Jungiansk teori og praksis i Danmark* (pp. 29–49). Copenhagen: Lindhardt og Ringhof.

FURTHER READING

Ainsworth, M. D. S., Blehar, M. C., Waters, E., & Wall, S. (1978). *Patterns of Attachment: A Psychological Study of the Strange Situation*. Hillsdale, NJ: Erlbaum.

Bower, T. G. R. (1977). *A Primer of Infant Development*. San Francisco: W. H. Freeman.

Bowlby, J. (1988). *A Secure Base. Clinical Applications of Attachment Theory*. London: Routledge.

Broberg, A., Granqvist, P. I., & Mothander, P. R. (2006). *Anknytningsteori*. Stockholm: Kultur & Natur.

Brodén, M. B. (1989). *Mor och barn i ingenmansland*. Solna: Almqvist & Wiksell.

Brodén, M. B. (2004). *Graviditetens möjligheter*. Stockholm: Natur & Kultur.

Dalhoff, A. (1998). *Cecilies verden*. Danish Doc Production. (Film about the life of Cecilie, a girl with Foetal Alcohol Syndrome).

Davis, M., & Wallbridge, D. (1981). *Boundary and Space. An Introduction to the Work of D. W. Winnicott*. New York, NY: Brunner-Routledge.

Davidsen-Nielsen, M., & Leick, N. (2004). *Den nødvendige smerte*. Copenhagen: Hans Reitzels Forlag.

Dolto, F. (1974). *Dominique: Analysis of an Adolescent*. London: Souvenir Press.

Dolto, F. & Severin, G. (1977). *L'Évangile au risque de la psychanalyse*. Paris: Jean-Pierre Délarge.

Dolto, F. (1985). *La cause des enfants*. Paris: Robert Laffont.

Dolto, F. (1988). *La cause des adolescents*. Paris: Robert Laffont.

Dolto, F. (1988). *Quand les parents se séparent*. Paris: Éditions du Seuil.

Gautré-Delay, F. (1997). *Interview med Caroline Eliacheff*. Agrippa, *18*: 224–232.

Glistrup, K. (2006). *Hvad børn ikke ved, har de ondt af. Familiesamtaler om psykisk lidelse*. Copenhagen: Hans Reitzels Forlag.

Glistrup, K. (2011). *Snak om angst og depression—med børn og voksne i alle aldre*. Copenhagen: Psykinfo Forlaget.

Gregersen, C. (2010). *Livsmod. Socialpædagogisk og psykoterapeutisk behandling af børn i Grønland*. Nuuk: Milik.

Heller, P. D., & Heller, S. L. (2001). *Crash Course. A Self-Healing Guide to Auto Accident Trauma and Recovery*. Berkeley, CA: North Atlantic Books.

Hostrup, H. (2010*). Gestalt Therapy: An Introduction to the Basic Concepts of Gestalt Therapy*. Copenhagen: Museum Tusculanum Press.

Jung, C. G. (2001). *Collected Works of C.G. Jung, Volume 7: Two Essays in Analytical Psychology*. Princeton, NJ: Princeton University Press.

Karsberg, S., Rønholt, S., & Elklit, A. (2012). *Hvordan identificerer og vurderer vi småbørnstraumer?* Odense: National Center of Psychotraumatology, University of Southern Denmark.

Levine, P. (1999). *Waking the Tiger: Healing Trauma*. Berkeley, CA: North Atlantic Books.

Levine, P. (2010). *In an Unspoken Voice. How the Body Releases Trauma and Restores Goodness*. Berkeley, CA: North Atlantic Books.

MacLean, P. (1990). *The Triune Brain in Evolution. Role in Paleocerebral Functions*. New York, NY: Plenum Press.

Mannoni, M. (1987). *Separation och utveckling—om brist, begär, språk och skapande*. Stockholm: Norstedts. [Original French edition (1982): D'un impossible à l'autre, Paris: Seuil.]

O'Toole, D. (1988). *Aarvy Aardvark Finds Hope*. Burnsville, NC: Compassion Books.

Poulsen, I., & Aagaard, G. (2012). Spædbarnsterapi. In: J. K. Høgsberg & H. Buch-Illing (Eds.), *Adoptionshåndbogen* (pp. 225–234). Copenhagen: Hans Reitzels Forlag.

Rosenbeck, A., & Thormann, I. (2000). *Når mor og far drikker*. Copenhagen: Hans Reitzels Forlag.

Rosenbeck, A., & Thormann, I. (2006). *Mor er psykisk syg*. Copenhagen: Hans Reitzels Forlag.

Rosenbeck, A., & Thormann, I. (2008). *Når mor og far slår*. Copenhagen: Hans Reitzels Forlag.

Rosenbeck, A., & Thormann, I. (2009). *Da Martins bedstefar døde*. Copenhagen: Hans Reitzels Forlag.

Rothschild, B. (2000). *The Body Remembers. The Psychophysiology of Trauma and Trauma Treatment*. New York, NY: Norton.

Schellenbaum, P. (1988). *Die Wunde der Ungeliebten*. Munich: Kösel.

Selva, D., & Coughlin, P. (1996). *Intensive Short-term Dynamic Psychotherapy*. London: Karnac.

Stern, D. (1977). *The First Relationship: Infant and Mother*. Boston: Harvard University Press.

Stern, D. (1990). *Diary of a Baby*. New York, NY: Basic Books.

Thormann, I. (2005). Omsorgssvigt. In: L. Hauge & M. Brørup (Eds.), *Gyldendals Psykologihåndbog* (pp. 78–96). Copenhagen: Gyldendal.

Thormann, I. (2009b). Den nænsomme overdragelse—om at få barnets liv til at hænge sammen. *Adoption og samfund*, 4: 12–13.

Thormann, I. (2011). Oplevelser med sprog. In: A. M. Marquardsen (Ed.), *Sprogmiljøer i børnehøjde* (pp. 29–36). Copenhagen: Dansk Psykologisk Forlag.

Thormann, I., & Branderup, R. (1992). *Hvor bliver du af mor*. Copenhagen: Hans Reitzels Forlag.

Thormann, I., & Branderup, R. (1997). *Thomas og Peter kommer i familiepleje*. Copenhagen: Hans Reitzels Forlag.

Thornsohn, S. (2010). *Alt usagt binder energi. En præsentation af Familiehuset i Horsens* (DVD).

Winnicott, D. W. (1965). *The Family and Individual Development*. London: Tavistock.

Winnicott, D. W. (1971). *Playing and Reality*. London: Tavistock.

Winnicott, D. W. (1987). *Babies and their Mothers*. London: Free Association Books.

Yalom, I. D. (1980). *Existential Psychotherapy*. New York, NY: Basic Books.

Yalom, I. D. (2001). *The Gift of Therapy: An Open Letter to a New Generation of Therapists and Their Patients*. New York, NY: Harper Collins.

INDEX

For Product Safety Concerns and Information please contact our EU
representative GPSR@taylorandfrancis.com
Taylor & Francis Verlag GmbH, Kaufingerstraße 24, 80331 München, Germany

9 781782 203094